Sybil Gregory

Begging for **REAL** Church

Dr. Joseph W. Daniels, Jr.
with Christine Shinn Latona

D0062052

BEACON OF LIGHT RESOURCES
WASHINGTON, DC

Begging for Real Church
Copyright © 2009 by Joseph W. Daniels, Jr.
All rights reserved.

ISBN: 978-0-9746759-5-4

No part of this book may be reproduced in any manner whatsoever without written
permission of the publisher except in brief quotations embodied in critical articles or
reviews. For information, write to:

Beacon of Light Resources
6128 Georgia Avenue, NW
Washington, DC 20011

Unless otherwise noted, scripture quotations were taken from the HOLY BIBLE, NEW
INTERNATIONAL VERSION®. Copyright © 1973, 1978, 1984 International Bible
Society. Used by permission of Zondervan. All rights reserved.

Scripture found on pages 98–99 was taken from THE MESSAGE. Copyright © 1993,
1994, 1995, 1996, 2000, 2001, 2002. Used by permission of NavPress Publishing
Group.

Credits for word definitions are found on page 128.

All of the life stories shared here are real but often the names and some specifics have
been altered in order to protect the confidentiality of the individual.

Cover Concept: Gary Shockley with Allie Plihal
Cover and Interior Design: KerseyGraphics

www.beggingforrealchurch.org
1.877.8b4.REAL

This book is dedicated to my father,

the late Joseph Wayne Daniels, Sr. and

my mother, Jeanne Adams Daniels.

Without the two of them I don't know where I'd be.

Thanks be to God for both of them.

I pray that this book blesses others in ways that

they have both blessed me.

We dedicate the profits from this book to grow real church in the Washington, DC area. The first million dollars in proceeds from this book will be used to fund The Beacon Center that will meet the needs of those begging for real church in the Brightwood community and beyond. Learn more at www.beggingforrealchurch.org.

Contents

Part 1 | Authentic Encounter — **18**

Part 2 | Meaningful Engagement — **50**

Part 3 | Radical Expectation   84

Acknowledgements

I discovered in a short period of time that there's no way a pastor can do effective ministry unless he has a loving, supportive and sacrificing family. God has blessed me with a tremendous one, and while I dedicate this book to my mom and dad who God used to give me life, I pause at the beginning of this book to acknowledge, recognize and thank the love of my life, my wife, my queen of 24 years, Madelyn Moore Daniels, who gives me strength. I truly don't know what my life would have come to, unless you decided to start walking with me intimately and intently some 30 years ago. Outside of Christ, you have been the rock of our marriage, the foundation of our home and the one who enables me to tick. There is no me without you.

To my wonderful daughter and son, Joia and Joey: God could not have blessed us with finer children. The joy you bring to our lives has no written or verbal description. I thank God for you, and for helping me to live a pastoral calling that always sees the importance to make and invest time in you and the family.

To Richard Bright and Samuel Mitchell, Jr., who got me started in this ministry thing. To my uncle Cornish Rogers, Bishop Marcus Matthews, Alphonso Harrod, David Jackson and all of them "Damn Daniels," who are the reason I'm in the United Methodist Church. To Mary Brown Oliver for taking a chance on me in June 1992.

To the Emory United Methodist Church, "The Emory Fellowship," I have been overwhelmingly blessed to pastor the greatest church in the world, and I am humbled and honored that God has given me this opportunity to share my life with you and yours. It has been a wonderful ride, and you have helped me get closer and closer to God through Jesus Christ. Your prayers, preaching support and persistent love have seen me through and the four-month sermon series on Real Church is the impetus for this book. Thank you is simply not enough.

I acknowledge my prayer partners, Vance P. Ross, Dred Scott, Tim Warner, Gary Henderson, Rudy Rasmus, Tyrone Gordon, Kevin Smalls and Hasker Samuel for their intentional prayers, friendship and brotherhood. Proverbs is true that "iron sharpens iron," and each of you continues to sharpen me in profoundly positive ways.

Thanks to Zan Wesley Holmes, Jr., the dean of preachers in the United Methodist Church, who has no idea the influence he has had on me and on the ministry God has entrusted me with. The statements at the beginning of each chapter are a reflection of him and his amazing ability to use words to convey complex realities with a simple turn of phrase.

Thanks to Carolyn Anderson and Larry and Nancy Shinn for their valuable constructive criticism, necessary edits and deep wisdom.

And last but not least, Christie Shinn Latona. God sent you to be the final antagonist to make me write, write and write some more. You are a great writer, inspired visionary and even better friend. The Lord bless you big time!

Foreword

Churches today face inordinate challenges. From long work hours through educational demands to infinite child athletic leagues, many are competitive options and opportunities. These stresses and strains scream for alternatives that bring relief.

In such an environment, where pressures can overwhelm any sense of joy, even of living, why even discuss church? If church refuses to address life in its perplexity, why bother?

Begging for Real Church responds to these questions. It offers an unusual church experience, an encounter that stands well outside the norm.

As a United Methodist church, this congregation defies normalcy, in that it has a pastor who has served more than 17 consecutive years. Emory and Joseph Daniels continue an ecclesiastical love affair that anchors the authentic recovery of a community and a people who claim Jesus as Lord of the universe, not merely those who actively ascribe to it. It is a church that could have been—that "should" have been—dead, buried and sold for its geographic and economic value: purchased as a ransom to silence a witness.

As a Black church, Emory stands in the Biblical tradition of diverse and inclusive ministry; all are invited and welcomed at this ministry table. However, this happens in a multicultural and international context. This Black church includes several Black accents and nationalities. It defies the typical understanding of American United Methodism: Black is a larger circle than African American. African, Latino, South American, Caribbean, Haitian and even those who would be described as White all find and call this congregation home.

Many "experts" say such a church cannot grow. In a church culture that fears distinction, adores homogeneity, quells spontaneity and enjoys inertia, this congregation differs. Unapologetically, it worships and works by the spiritual disciplines. Aggressively, Emory invites persons across class, color and culture lines. Expectantly, the congregation looks for the "move of God," fearlessly seeking evidence. Assertively, these people act to change the community.

In Emory, God proves different than the experts say. Once a District Superintendent assignment, Emory now has a growing church staff. Once a church expected to die, it now serves as a model congregation for vitality and vigor. Once a church for which expectations were low and possibilities were even lower, it is now a large United Methodist Congregation. Once a church clergy wanted no part of, it now claims a pulpit where the finest of preachers desire—even ask—for the opportunity to proclaim the Gospel.

How has this happened? This has happened by the grace and power of God who—in and through the person of Jesus—has so infected a ministry with a Holy Spirit virus that it compels its people to share the healing and wholeness so often ignored by churches. The sophisticated, elevated politeness that keeps so many churches from knowing, loving and caring for others is not seen here. Emory Church lives a divergent way, a distinctive life and an unusual commitment.

Joseph W. Daniels, Jr. has been my prayer partner for over 11 years. As Emory grows, supporting and challenging its adherents and the community, I marvel at how he continues to call his people to look to God for what is real. Authenticity prevails over all issues and concerns. He leads this church to practice the reality of prayer and fasting, to dare the arduous labor of spiritual study and to center all ministries—small and large group—in the presence and worship of God through Jesus, always expecting transformation.

Make no mistake: this has not been an easy road. Challenges have come in many forms and persons. Situations emanating from both the brilliant and the beleaguered often make personal and corporate ministry hazardous, if not entirely dangerous. Yet, Pastor Daniels and Emory remain a people and a place of joy. For Emory, validity finds itself in blessings more than in burdens, in grace more than in grief.

This text is about God's blessings and grace, about the joy of this ministry. Joseph Daniels and Christie Latona share a gift of honest and sincere congregational love, and struggle and work with the many gifted disciples of Jesus called the Emory Fellowship. This is more than a "wished for" or "dreamed of" congregation. This is what God has done and thus what God can do. It is what can happen when a pastor and a people recognize that communities *"Begging for Real Church"* need real churches. Read this, then dare your church to be real as well.

Vance P. Ross
Deputy General Secretary for
The General Board of Discipleship
of The United Methodist Church
and Pastoral Staff, Hobson United
Methodist Church, both in Nashville, TN

Introduction

For years, in fact for most of my life, I have been begging for real church. But it wasn't until 16 years into my ministry that I attempted to capture what real church is for myself and for those gathered for worship. Drawing on my life experiences, church experiences and pastoral experiences, I embarked upon a sermon series called "Real Church." What started out as a standard six-week series expanded into an exhaustive, yet introductory, four-month experience. On the Sundays where I just couldn't deal with it all, I thank God for Sherwyn Benjamin and Henry Stewart, who preached and walked with me throughout the series.

So what is "real church?" Simply put, a "real church" is an authentic, transparent and real collection of sinners saved by grace, who aren't afraid to tell their life stories, share their life challenges and point one another to a way of life that helps overcome all obstacles: a life walking with Jesus. A life filled with challenges and transformations, with tests and blessings, with times of wilderness and of deliverance.

A real church is spiritually mature, alert, perceptive and discerning. It is one that isn't afraid to push people where they need to be pushed, to rebuke when in need of rebuking, and all the while loving unconditionally like everybody needs to be loved. As a friend of ours says, "We love you just the way you are, but too much to let you stay there."

Extending this unconditional love propels a real church. Love propels real church to flexibly equip people of all conditions in ways they need equipping. Love propels real church to receive, prepare and position people to serve in the places and spaces where their service could best be used—all in the name of Jesus and by the power of the Holy Ghost!

Show me somebody who is begging for real church and I'll show you someone who is begging for an authentic encounter. Show me somebody who is begging for real church and I'll show you someone who desires to be meaningfully engaged in something greater than themselves. Show me somebody who is begging for real church and I'll show you someone who expects a better life. Show me somebody who *finds* real church and I'll show you someone whose life is alive and positioned to be a blessing to the world.

Show me a real church and I'll show you folks who used to beg full-time, who are now learning how to exchange begging for blessing. We are beggars telling other beggars how to find the Bread of Life; beggars who continue the search for an even deeper, more challenging and even discomforting experience of real church.

And so, as we start this journey, the people we're hoping to reach in this book are beggars. Not just the typical beggar we encounter with frequency in any urban, suburban and rural context—not just a man or woman from a major metropolitan area looking for a handout, or trying to run a scam on you—but a beggar like you and me. Someone who wants so much more than what life seems to be offering right now; someone who feels stuck—unable to move—towards the plans and purposes they've dreamed of, imagined and even heard God speak to them; someone whose hopes and aspirations have ended up in disappointment so many times, that they've just come to accept the crumbs, the leftovers of life.

> Beggars beg for wholeness in many different dimensions— physically, emotionally, spiritually, socially and financially.

In real life, there are parallels between both of the beggars outlined above. A beggar is someone in need. A beggar has real or perceived defects that prevent him or her from accessing power. A beggar is captive to someone or something—unable to move. A beggar is someone who is in need of a life-transforming experience. Beggars beg for wholeness in many different dimensions—physically, emotionally, spiritually, socially and financially. A beggar is a beggar is a beggar. Searching for something that is greater than what can be provided in handouts.

It is oftentimes hard to admit, but most of us have been in a begging situation before. Begging for that fantastic relationship. Begging for that awesome job or promotion. Begging for peace, harmony and love in a family that has not achieved it yet. Begging for prosperity that positions us to be a blessing to someone else. The list could go on and on. Most of us have been beggars before or are beggars right now.

Many people have turned to the church to provide answers to the human condition of our begging. Historically, Americans have gone to church. However, in the past decade or so, the numbers of people faithfully attending a church community have dwindled significantly, with worship attendance on an average weekend experienced by less than 20% of the population.

I would argue these numbers have dwindled because in coming to church, the vast majority have not and are not receiving a real experience, nor are they getting answers or teachings that will liberate them from their begging conditions. The songs being sung are simply not speaking to their current reality. The Word being preached is irrelevant to their daily needs, or indeed to that which is causing them to beg. To make matters worse, the interaction between people in many of our churches lacks authenticity. In many churches today we are more concerned with ritual and routine than we are with helping people at their point of need—whether that need be physical, emotional, mental, relational, financial or spiritual.

> We are more concerned with ritual and routine than we are with helping people at their point of need

There is a silent yet resounding cry for "real church"—a space and place where genuine relationships with God and one another can be created so that our dreams, hopes, visions and destinies can become realities.

In the story of *Acts 3,* two men—one named Peter and one named John—encounter this man outside the front of the church begging for money. He's been there a long time. In fact, he has been begging at the church for 40 long years. Every day he was brought by somebody to the church steps to beg for money because he was lame—unable to move independently—from birth.

In those days people with defects weren't allowed to go to church… even though the church was thought to be the place for healing, the place for the answers to our questions. But each day someone brought this guy to the front door of the church, perhaps with the hopes that someone would take him inside so that he could be healed. After 40 years, this man had become accustomed to daily disappointment. But in the story we learn that Peter and John, on their way to church, gave the beggar what he was really looking for.

Peter and John see this guy and he prepares to ask them for money, but little did the beggar know Peter and John were about to give him something that this man probably hoped for and dreamed of, but never thought was possible. And that was the ability to walk, move, be and do all the things he hoped for to live a more full life. Peter and John gave this beggar an authentic encounter with Jesus the Christ, and the beggar's life was never the same. They did so by first meaningfully engaging him. They told the beggar, "Look at us!" Then they shifted his expectations when they said, "Silver and gold we do not have, but what we have we give you. In the name of Jesus Christ of Nazareth, walk!"[1] This expectation led to the beggar leaping up and praising God. The beggar proved to the world that a real church experience is available to all—even to beggars.

Once the beggar got up running, leaping and praising God, he along with Peter and John, entered the church building. It was a statement and action, suggesting and later revealing, that the folks inside the church really needed what the beggar outside had received: A life changing experience in Jesus Christ!

> There are beggars like these all through scripture, and there are beggars like these in our world.

This beggar isn't the only beggar in scripture looking for a real church experience. Beggars are all throughout scripture. They are the widow at Zarephath needing more food before she and her son die. They are the Shunemmite woman who has everything she could materially want, but has a poor marriage and a dead son and is looking for restoration. They are King David who compromised his relationship with God because he couldn't keep his zipper up. They are the man blind from birth that Jesus gave sight. They are the hemorrhaging woman who touched the hem of Jesus' garment, found that her bleeding had stopped, was compelled to testify and found that her faith had made her well. They are the prodigal son who had it all, left it all, and found that even in his failure, Jesus loved him anyhow. There are beggars like these all through scripture, and there are beggars like these in our world. In wealthy and poor circles, in those marginalized and those exalted, in middle class neighborhoods and gated communities.

In this book we hope to provide the spiritual nourishment—Holy Ghost food and drink—so that present-day beggars everywhere might have a taste of a real church experience and know that it is possible to exchange begging for blessing.

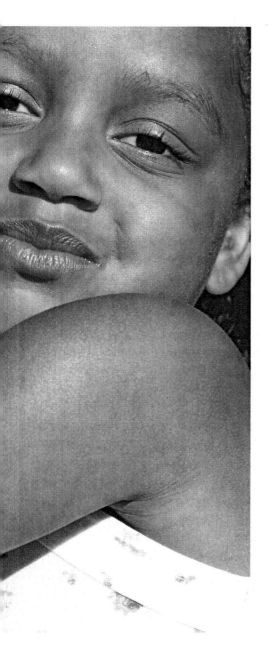

Part 1

Authentic Encounter

To live a life where challenges lead to transformations requires an authentic encounter. An authentic encounter with others in the name of Jesus opens the door for wisdom, understanding and pathways to holistic living.

Authentic \ə-'then-tik, ó-\ **1.** worthy of acceptance or belief as conforming to or based on fact **2.** conforming to an original so as to reproduce essential features **3.** made or done the same way as an original **4.** not false or imitation: real, actual

The human desire for authenticity transcends cultures and time. Those who have been burned, betrayed or fooled may have their BS (belief sensing) radar up at all times. And they should. The chapters in this section seek to provide a worthy and real encounter that will help you discover what you need to do in order to be open to the notion of being healed.

Encounter \in-'kaùn-tər, en-\ **1.** to engage in conflict with **2.** to come upon face-to-face **3.** to come upon or experience especially unexpectedly **4.** to meet especially by chance

Now why in the world would we include the notion of conflict in the definition of encounter? Because an authentic encounter in the name of Jesus won't necessarily be comfortable—there will be a disturbance. A disturbance of how we typically think, believe and feel. But an authentic encounter with Jesus will be therapeutic; will bring peace of mind, body and soul; will transform us in ways we need and desire.

Everyday we are faced with opportunities to experience, unexpectedly, the hand of God. This authentic encounter is the first key step in transforming our begging to blessing.

Chapter 1
What Are You Begging For?

Show me a real church and I will show you a church who still actively seeks to exchange begging for blessing. Show me a real church and I will show you a people who know and can tell you first hand what it means to beg and what they used to beg for.

When we take a good look at the beggar in *Acts 3,* he exposes, without saying a word, his daily human reality. He has been lame from birth. We later find out that he has been lame for 40 years.

To be lame is to be paralyzed…unable to move. So the immediate picture we get of this man is that he's crippled. He's unable to move his limbs. He cannot walk or get around on his own. He is dependent upon others to get from point "A" to point "B."

Taking it further, he can dream, but he can't accomplish his dreams. He can have a vision, but he can't pursue his vision. He can hope, but his condition describes one who is hopeless. For him, every day is the same old rhyme and routine. He goes through the same old motions, expecting handouts, but not expecting anything that can actually change him.

Robert Williams has been looking for something more since middle school. If it wasn't help with getting homework done that he was too lazy to complete, then it was begging for lunch money. Almost every day Robert would ask his friends for lunch money.

Robert has a heart of gold. Throughout our childhood and adolescence, he dreamed big dreams of playing college basketball successfully. A part of his dream included being positioned to help disadvantaged kids turn their lives around and having a prosperous life. Even though Robert has been true to a part of his dream by spending most of his adult years working with disabled children, he hasn't fully reached what he could have because he's been stuck, unable to move. His paralysis is caused by being comfortable with what he has: laziness, mediocrity, a drinking habit, an up-and-down and on-again-off-again marriage and other traps that have restricted him from his dreams.

There are many people in this world—inside and outside the church—who dream big, but cannot reach their dreams. Who have a vision, but can't see their way forward. Who hope, but who (like the song writer James Weldon Johnson) suffer from hope unborn that has died. They never get to what *can* be, let alone what God promises **will** be with just a little faith.

You may be the person I'm describing or maybe just a part of your life is lame. You've dreamed of being a teacher, but couldn't afford the education to get there. You've imagined becoming a doctor, but one failed test stopped you from pursuing your goal. You wanted to be a broadcaster, but, like me, classmates told you that you talk too slowly.

Maybe for you the lameness is centered on being stuck in a relationship. Maybe you long for a partner who will love you for who you are, who will accept and support you for who you wish to be or for someone who doesn't hurt you or blame you for things that aren't in your control.

Maybe for you the lameness is something else. You've been stuck there for a long time. And all of the signs of being stuck seem to surround you. Financial debt, drug addiction, alcohol addiction, sex addiction, low self-esteem, depression, anxiety, fear and the like all seem to hover around you, hold you and refuse to let you go.

If I'm talking about you, don't feel bad. You are not alone. I don't know about you, but I have been lame before. I have found myself depressed and unable to move after the death of my father. I have

found myself afraid to succeed even though I had the giftedness and a
mother who daily encouraged me to succeed. I have run away from the
people who told me I could, and instead hung out with people who
said I couldn't. Or with those who believed that because they couldn't,
I couldn't either. I have made bad financial moves. I have flirted with
drugs and alcohol. I know what it means to be anxious, empty and
wondering what tomorrow will bring, let alone later today.

I've been stuck. It is no fun being stuck. It is no fun being unable to
move. Life becomes boring, routine, frustrating, monotonous, dull and
strangely comfortable.

That's what life was for Eddie Harris. We ran into Eddie on the
street corner. He was drunk, cantankerous,
homeless and making trouble. A nuisance to
society and himself. He was begging. In his
case he was begging for food and for money
to buy beer and alcohol. But what he really
wanted, but didn't believe was possible, was a
fresh start at life.

> They never get to what can be, let alone what God promises **will** be

Eddie had had a successful career in
the military. Well into this stellar career he
was accused of a crime he did not commit.
He was chosen as the scapegoat because of the color of his skin and
humiliated by his reporting officers. Their disrespect sent him into a
rage, and his rage resulted in a dishonorable discharge. His salary and
benefits were stripped from him. Within a short period of time, he went
from an honorable soldier to a homeless veteran. His last stint in prison
was the result of a lethal combination of alcohol, temper and violence
that nearly killed a car full of people. Racism, anger and temptation left
him lame and unable to move. Stuck on the streets in a drunken stupor,
Eddie didn't even know what he was begging for.

Laurie came from a family who loved her, but who never really
rooted that love in faith or in hugs. Her parents were emotionally
detached from one another and the children. Her own sense of worth
was always tied up in how she looked, how she behaved and how she
performed in school, sports and music. As an adult Laurie battled with
alcoholism, depression and anxiety. She judges others so that she might

feel better about herself. She puts other people's kids down for stuff her own children do. She fights with her husband and her son non-stop on a wide range of topics. Laurie is begging for peace of mind, love, family harmony and deliverance from self-loathing.

Desiree comes from a very proud family. A family where there is great accomplishment and notoriety. But a dysfunctional family with a lot of issues and brokenness that ranges from drug abuse to alcohol addiction to incest and abuse. Desiree is the oldest of four kids. Like many victims of abuse, Desiree got married to a man who continued the cycle of abuse. She struggled with health issues that made it difficult to have children and suffered from several miscarriages. Her husband wouldn't stop drinking, using drugs and abusing her. With so much pressure in their lives from broken dreams and bad habits, their marriage broke apart at the seams, leaving Desiree and her husband in deep depressions—no child, no marriage, no healthy family life. Desiree and her lost husband are begging. Desiree is broken many times over. She is begging for a healthy child, a healthy relationship with a man and ultimately a healthy family life.

> A lot of people get comfortable with being lame.

A lot of people get comfortable with being lame. Sometimes it is more comfortable to be lame because escaping a stuck situation is difficult. Sometimes, the longer you are lame the less you think a change is necessary, and the burden of the condition takes away any energy you might have to actually get out. Sometimes, by the time you decide you want out of a stuck situation, you are left powerless and begging for a way out.

As the story of *Acts 3* unfolds, we find this lame man is simply left to beg on a daily basis. He is begging just to survive. He is begging for food to eat, money to give to those who are taking care of him and money to meet his daily obligations. We can imagine that what he really wants is to walk for the first time, no longer be dependent on others. But walking is completely out of the scope of his imagination.

Are you begging for a place to stay because you are homeless or because you are living in a house you really don't want to be in? Are you begging for peace of mind, body and soul? Are you begging for a good job that will pay you a good salary so that money will not be the main thing on your mind, but instead a means for you to achieve the goals you dream about daily? Do you beg for a good relationship that could lead to courtship, friendship or maybe even marriage? Are you begging for something different from anything and everything that is real in your life right now? Are you begging for someone to just be able to hear and feel your pain? To sit with you for a little while in your pain and perhaps, even help get you out of your pain?

What are you begging for?

Time to Be REAL
(Relevant, Enthusiastic, Authentic and Loving)

Take a few minutes now to capture your reactions to what you have just read. You don't need a fancy journal. You don't need anything but some time and something to write with and on. This may be difficult for you at first because many of us are closet beggars...we haven't admitted to others or ourselves what we need. And we aren't used to doing anything constructive to change our situation.

❶ Whose story do you relate to the most? How does this compare and contrast with your story?

❷ What are things that you really, really want that are outside of your scope of reality? Start writing or typing three unedited pages now. Pour it all out.

Make sure each statement is connected to your daily reality. For example: "respect" could become "a friend who really listens to me when I talk to him/her."

❸ Read through all that you've written. In one sentence, state what you are really begging for:

I am begging for _____so
that I might_____.

Chapter 2
Where Are You Begging?

Show me a real church and I'll show you a church that radically extends its heart and hands to beggars. Show me a real church and I'll show you a people who understand the plight of beggars and are concerned with their well-being.

People beg in a lot of places. The street corner in the center of any major city is not the sole place of begging. People beg for loans in banks, for leniency in the courtroom. People beg for forgiveness in marriage, a second chance with children. People beg for mercy in all types of places. But in this quest to find what it is that your life is missing, where are you begging?

For the beggar in *Acts 3* who is looking for food and money to survive, the temple was the place to go because the temple in his day was the center of community life. Not only was it a place of worship, but it was also a place of business transactions, trading, investing, relationship building, socializing, entertaining, status, power, position and prestige. In this man's day, if you were cut off from the temple, you were cut off from life.

And so the natural place for someone to bring him to beg was the "church" of his day. At church, people would pass by and give him at least the bare minimum that he begged for. At church, people with means to help him would pass by and share their means with him. At church, people with the material resources would drop some of their crumbs to help him along the way. However, the temple (the church) would not offer him what he really needed because the people who went to this temple were not really concerned with the man's well-being. They were content with doing whatever was necessary to get this man off of their conscience. They were content with giving a handout to this man, not a lift up.

> A lot of people have been locked out of perceived places of power, places where people believe that positive change can happen.

Furthermore this temple, this "church," which was institutional in nature, would not let the beggar inside, where the healing of a fellowship might have transformed him. He had a defect: he was lame. And a known defect was a sign and signal to others in his day that you were a sinner; that you were cursed of God, not blessed; that you had done something wrong; that you had to get some things right with God before you could be a part of this church. And so the institutional church, the temple in the text, would lock you out.

A lot of people have been locked out of perceived places of power, places where people believe that positive change can happen. Locked out because we have a defect that the institutional church deems unworthy for our entrance into the place where our healing can begin.

Have you ever been locked out of the church before? I have. I remember at the age of 20, my great friend Hasker Samuel, who is now the keyboardist at The Emory Fellowship, and I petitioned the leaders of the church where we spent our teenage years to have a Bible study for the young people. In fact, we wanted to lead it. But because of our ages, and because the trustees did not want to open the doors for us to have the study at the time we designated, we were locked out of this opportunity to learn and study God. We were at a critical age in our lives and we realized that those we wanted to study with were there, too. We were fighting temptation. We were seeking to find our own identity. We were trying to settle on a career path. We were seeking to get our collective acts together as we begged for true meaning in life, begged for direction and begged for purpose. And the institutional church, like the temple, locked us out.

The only place we see in the story of *Acts 3* where this beggar can go for help is the institutional church because, in the story, we have no references to this beggar having access to any other historical institutions. We are not told that he has a family; so obviously healing love, care, and support did not come from his family. We are not told if he has any friends, only that he has people who bring him to the temple and then desert him every day. These friends are obviously powerless when it comes to ushering him into a life-change on their own. We do not get the picture that the beggar is a part of any fraternity, sorority or civic organization, community group or club. He is all by himself. Locked out from the one place that God said should be able to provide him healing.

Like this beggar, many of us have been locked out of places of healing and power. Locked out of our families, places of employment, schools, social clubs, associations and/or other places where lasting friendships and healing connections can be formed. And as a result, we have sought to find help and healing in other places.

We seek to find help in places where helpless people gather. Places where alcohol replaces authenticity, and unconditional sex replaces unconditional love. Places where greed replaces grace, where putting down replaces lifting up. Places where a quest for material wealth replaces the journey toward true riches. Places where violence replaces understanding, and people have no common faith or community to overcome crises as they arise. And so when you are locked out, where do you go?

Eddie was locked out of the military institution that removed access to a salary, a pension and health care. He was stripped of his capacity to thrive. No place to live, no place to work and he had to relearn skills to help him get a job even though what he had learned in the military was transferable. Eddie went to the street to find what he was begging for.

Desiree sought relationships with others who had lost so much that they were consumed by anger and indignation. She was not finding the answers she needed with God and the church. She reached a point where, if God is God, then why? She was left begging in the places and spaces where people asking, "Why God?" gather. Those places are often out of the realm and the reach of those who can actually help. The people, the proclamation, the power and the presence of God seemed distant to her.

Laurie begs in environments where alcohol flows and many people are gathered who will participate in gossiping and putting others down.

> Where is the place you can go to find the people to help you bring your begging to an end?

Where have you gone to find what you are begging for? Many go to Starbucks for Sunday brunch only to be left with an empty cup when they are finished. Some go to football games, live or on TV, to try and escape the pain (only to find more pain when their favorite team loses). Others of us go to golf courses, tennis courts, card games, shopping malls, fashion shows or faraway destinations, casinos, lottery lines, or race tracks—looking, hoping, begging for that one thing we are missing. Only to be left empty because what we are really looking for, or what we really need—a life changing encounter with Jesus Christ—is not typically found in these places of begging.

Once you are in a begging environment, it is very hard to get out of it. Usually you find yourself in a place with other people who are powerless in the same way that you are, or with other people who want what you want, who need what you need, but who don't know how to get it in healthy and life-sustaining ways.

Where is the place you can go to find the people to help you bring your begging to an end? Robert goes to the six-pack every opportunity possible. Eddie went to the street and the people in the street couldn't help him because they were on the street just like he was. Desiree ran to people and places who were broken like she was and who had no answers for her shattered state. Laurie tried unsuccessfully to take matters into her own hands. When will we learn that our hands aren't enough to handle things that are beyond our control? All of these places of begging may provide short-term solace, but they lack the long-term liberation that all beggars long for.

If you feel like churches are a place for saints and you feel like less than a saint, then you will never go to a church to beg. It is time for real churches to make it clear that beggars are welcome. The Emory Fellowship where I pastor is one such church. They actively proclaim that we are real church for real people. We aren't a perfect church, but we are seeking to be a real expression of welcome and healing for the beggar. An example of this is our noon service on Sunday. It is here where the wealthy, middle class, homeless and people on the street gather together, cry together, laugh together, worship together, hug each other and help one another. Afterwards they share a meal, find and provide clothing, look for job opportunities and the like. All in an effort to help each other become whole, individually and as a community—as a church.

Transformation is possible if we allow ourselves to transparently beg in places that seek to heal in the name of Jesus.

Time to Be REAL
(Relevant, Enthusiastic, Authentic and Loving)

On a piece of paper, make three columns:

1 I am begging for...	**2** I am begging for it here...	**3** I rate the transforming power of the help that I'm getting there...

Fill in your columns by answering the following questions:

❶ What are you begging for? In the first column insert your answers from the exercise in Chapter 1.

❷ Where are you begging for it? In the second column, make note of ALL of the locations, situations and people you are begging for help.

❸ What kind of help are you getting? Honestly assess the degree to which your places of begging will yield transformation. Use a scale of 1–10 where
   a. 1 = encourages me to stay in my begging state
   b. 5 = feels like there might be a way out
   c. 10 = has the power to transform my begging into a blessing

Chapter 3
Do You Feel Your Help Comin'?

Show me a real church and I will show you a church that looks to help people move from a life of begging to a life of blessing. Show me a real church and I will show you a people who trust that with God nothing is impossible.

God helps beggars like you and me find what we really need by sending ordinary people, who carry God's extraordinary power, into our everyday circumstances to lead us to extraordinary miracles. Miracles that then lead us to worship God in spirit and truth, and serve God through meeting the needs of others—just like our needs were met. The only way the beggar in the story finds healing is when two ordinary people, possessed with extraordinary power, refuse to pass him by.

When I was begging for a holistic life as a young adult in Houston, Texas, I sought for it in promiscuous parties, betraying bedrooms and brew company kegs. God sent a miracle in the form of a young adult by the name of Emery Biro, who was ready to share real church.

Emery was an ordinary guy, a short white boy I met in a class one day, who had a bright smile, great sense of humor and a genuine personality. We gravitated to one another because he was a student athlete at Rice University in Houston, just like I was. He played tennis;

I played basketball. But he was from Maryland just the same—me from Silver Spring, he from the state capitol of Annapolis. Being 1,500 miles away from home, finding a "homeboy" was a connection—a connection that would prove divine.

Emery made it known from the start that he was building a relationship with this man named Jesus. I wasn't scared when he told me; I'd been raised in church all of my life and heard about this man named Jesus. But what I quickly found out was that just like a man dates a woman and a woman dates a man, seeking to get to know one another in deep and perhaps intimate ways, Emery was trying to get to know Jesus, the Savior of the world, in a deeper, more intimate way. And soon, he invited me to do the same.

He invited me to a group called Fellowship of Christian Athletes, which ended up forming a basketball team Bible study that Emery, a tennis player, joined in. I invited him to lift weights with me during the offseason in the football stadium weight room. Every now and then, we'd get up early on Sunday morning and go to this boring church down the street from campus so that I could at least tell my mom that I had fulfilled my Sunday obligation. We were building a connection.

Up to that point, our lives converged in the weight room and the Bible study, but went in separate directions afterwards. While Emery tried his best to walk right, I had become content with living what I called "a dual lifestyle." I showed the "holy" side to Emery when I was with him—I lived the "wild" side in his absence. I'd come to study on Sunday evening, and then spend the night studying women in their bedrooms. I'd talk with Emery and others about the Christ, and then go find a "cooler" at the campus party so that I could quickly and deeply catch a buzz. I'd mention Jesus every now and then, but then occasionally allow myself to be in predicaments with people where guilt by association could have easily taken me to jail. This dual lifestyle was threatening to kill me, and my change wasn't coming from the Sunday morning worship. It wasn't coming from the Sunday evening Bible study. Change started coming when God sent an ordinary person with God's extraordinary power to my dual lifestyle circumstance to lead me to an extraordinary miracle—a life change that would lead me from the road of destruction to the road of redemption, restoration and revival.

One day in February 1980, Emery and I were lifting weights. When we'd finished lifting and were walking back to our rooms, Emery made a simple statement and then asked me a question. "Joe, I thought you said you are a Christian." I told him, "I am." He then asked, "Well then why don't you act like it?" I wanted to bust him in the head, but the fact that he had connected with me, spent time with me and showed a genuine concern for my well-being—real church characteristics—defused my anger and forced me to deal with the statement and question. And right there, in that empty football stadium parking lot, I heard the sound of cheering from a countless multitude in heaven because a wayward soul named Joe Daniels realized that life had something better to offer, and that something better could be found in walking with Jesus.

I don't remember what my response was to Emery. Although I kept walking with him back to the main part of campus, my mind, my thoughts and my energies were in another world. I was smiling, I was enthusiastic, I was overwhelmingly eager to give up some old stuff that I was shameful of and start a new life that this man named Jesus told me I could freely have. I felt my help comin'. From being called a "tramp" by one woman, I could now see the pathway to a triumphant life. From a fearful existence of dancing with the devil, I began receiving glimpses of a glorious destiny for my life. From being paralyzed by shame and suffering from sin that had made me lame, unable to move, God was shining in me and showing me a new mosaic of life's opportunities and possibilities that the Master would orchestrate. God had shown up in my suffering with a miracle—through an ordinary person carrying God's extraordinary power, who didn't mind showing it or sharing it at the God-ordained and God-inspired time. My help came!

In the story of the beggar, Peter and John, fresh off their excitement over a move of God that changed their lives for the better, decide that

> We stop and help people in their time of need, EVEN if it means that our own agendas have to be adjusted.

they will go to the temple to worship. On their way there, they run into this man, lame from birth, begging at the temple gates. Because God was active and alive in their lives, having visited them in their time of need, Peter and John, seeing a brother in need, stopped, rather than pass by. This is a critical aspect of real church—we stop and help people in their time of need, EVEN if it means that our own agendas have to be adjusted. Emery Biro stopped his life for a moment to include mine in his. And both of our lives have never been the same again.

Whenever we move for God and with God because we possess God, miraculous things will happen. Peter and John get to the temple with the intent of worshipping God inside. But instead, they have an encounter with the beggar in the name of Jesus and worship God outside the church. The lives of hurting people change when the lives of those who have been healed slow down for five minutes and offer a transformative hand and/or word, and help transform the life of a hurting soul.

As the story continues, Peter and John command this man's attention, and instead of giving him what he wants, Peter and John give him what he needs. Does he need money? Yes. Does he need food? Yes. Does he need to take care of the material needs of survival? Yes. But more than that, he needs to get up and walk because he's stuck in a situation that's incapacitating, and he needs to be able to get out of it.

> Just a simple helping hand from an ordinary person with God's extraordinary power can turn around someone's life forever.

If he can get up and walk, he will then have the capacity to do all the things he hoped for or dreamed of. If he can get up and walk, he can leave the frustration and get to the fundamental things of a holistic life. That's his real need: to get up and walk. In order for this need to be met he needs the extraordinary power of Jesus. For in his 40 years of paralysis, and who knows how many years of begging, there has been nothing humanly available to heal him. Knowing that, Peter and John, the Emery Biros of their day, give him the one thing that they themselves know can heal, and that is the extraordinary power of Jesus. How is Jesus shared with them? Peter gives the man his hand and commands him in the name of Jesus (and the power he has) to get up. He then lifts him from paralysis to possibility. Just a simple helping hand from an ordinary person with God's extraordinary power can turn around someone's life forever. That hand caused the man to not only get up, but it also caused him to be able to stand, to leap, to walk and to give God praise. His life would never be the same again.

There are so many in this world that want to be helped like this. Yet there are so many barriers that have kept people from getting this help. There are so many people who don't know that real church is this simple, and begins this simply. First of all, so many people have never experienced anyone seeking to share the extraordinary power of Jesus. Secondly, so many people don't believe that Jesus can do what He said He would do. They don't believe that He can heal us from begging situations. Thirdly, religious institutions have focused more on self-preservation than on the deliverance of people from the shackles that keep so many of us bound—spiritual shackles, emotional shackles, mental shackles, relational shackles, financial shackles, all kinds of shackles. As a result, we are not whole *nor do we think we can be.*

Allen Jones is a leader of the church who took his church obligations very seriously but who was a hypocrite. He was in shackles. He professed to know God on one hand, but on the other hand, he would anger church members by walking past them without speaking. Allen sang in the choir almost every Sunday, singing the songs of Zion, yet he would be found at numerous parties dancing feverously, drinking uncontrollably and womanizing like the worst of them. By his own admission, Allen was a drunk and a womanizer—behaviors that for years tarnished his name, tarnished his family's name and caused great pain and consternation amongst his family, friends and associates. Allen was begging for a restored reputation, for sobriety and for stable and authentic relationships.

Allen went to a men's conference with a group from his church. The workshop he attended was the vehicle God used to take Allen by the hand from his begging state and lift him to a place where his life would be transformed forever. Allen came out of that workshop "lit," not from alcohol this time, but from the Holy Ghost. The conference ended on a Saturday night in Florida. Allen was so passionate about being in worship the next day that he and the men drove straight through the night so that he might stand up and testify during Sunday worship. And on that Sunday morning in October, Allen stood in front of his wife and the congregation to declare that his past life of drunkenness, womanizing, partying and carousing was over. On that day he made a commitment to God and before God to his wife, congregation and God that he was going to follow Jesus Christ and that they had a right to hold him accountable to his word.

> What we all need is to find ourselves in a climate where the possibilities of an all-powerful God can come to pass

That was ten years ago and he has not looked back. In fact, he is now reaching out his hand to lift up men who are in the same begging state he used to be in.

What we all need is to find ourselves in a climate where the possibilities of an all-powerful God can come to pass in our lives through the very people that God, through Jesus Christ, has blessed in our midst. People like the divorcee who, by the grace and power of God, has overcome the pain of her divorce and is now positioned to help others overcome theirs. People like the drunk who has found sobriety in Jesus and is now positioned to tell his story so that other drunks can be delivered. People like those once greedy and gluttonous for all of the world's material riches. People, who in being broke, busted, disgusted, heavily in debt and destructed, have found a Deliverer who provides riches with no price tag. People like the doctor, who in all of her medical training discovers that after she has done all she can do, God is still there to heal. People like the lawyer, who after defending the client with his own acquired legal skills discerns that he needs "justice to roll down like waters and righteousness like an ever flowing stream." People like the whoremonger and the gigolo, who in spite of living lives and sharing their bodies with whoever would pay the tab, now realize that their bodies mean something to God, and therefore commit themselves to help others realize that they can be loved in healthy ways.

When a climate like this is created, get ready to see the healing, life-changing and joy-producing power that Jesus is ready to unleash in our lives.

Our help comes when God sends ordinary people with God's extraordinary power to our every day circumstances to lead us to extraordinary miracles, grounded in the power of Jesus. Who might be positioned in your life to extend you a hand in the name of Jesus?

Do you feel your help comin'?

Time to Be REAL
(Relevant, Enthusiastic, Authentic and Loving)

❶ What rang true for you in this chapter?

❷ Reflect on what it would take for you to be ready to trade begging for a blessing.
- Would it take you terminating a bad relationship so you can begin a healthy one?
- Would it require you to stop spending money you don't have and to start learning the principles of sound financial management?
- Would you need to forgive somebody that you have refused to forgive that has resulted in a bitterness that eats you alive?
- Would it mean that you start loving somebody who has been very hard to love?
- Would it mean that you take a risk that you know you need to take, but have been afraid to take for so many years?
- Would it mean that you would trust somebody who has proven trustworthy, even though you've been burned too many times?
- Would it take believing in God for the very first time?
- Would it take trusting and obeying God for the very first time?
- Would it take trusting someone else for the very first time?

❸ Commit to do one thing right now (or to STOP doing one thing right now) to create a climate where the possibilities of an all-powerful God can come to pass in your life. Write down that commitment, put the date on it, put it in an envelope and seal it. Give it to a person you trust and ask them to give it back to you in 30 days.

❹ In the meantime, identify the ordinary person in your life who might be positioned to give you a hand in the name of Jesus. Ask God to help you be open.

Chapter 4
Is Trust a Four-Letter Word?

Show me a real church and I will show you a church where the people are willing to trust Jesus and trust one another. Show me a real church and I'll show you a people who are transparent with one another.

Trusting others is a critical part of having an authentic encounter with Jesus. If the beggar didn't have an ounce of trust in Peter, he would have rebelled against Peter lifting him, let alone having a conversation with him or looking at him. So many of us miss our help because we refuse to trust. I would have missed my life change if I didn't trust the message of the Lord sent through Emery Biro in that football parking lot in February of 1980. And we refuse to trust because we've been burned so many times by people we thought could help us or should help us. People like pastors, church leaders, doctors, lawyers and even parents.

Some of the people who have hurt me the most have been pastors and church folks. They have stolen money from me, made sexual advances toward me, made statements to hurt my family and even harassed my character and integrity. I really believe the reason a lot of people stay away from church is because they've been hurt in church, and not seen a church with this authentic, transparent and real attitude in the people—an attitude and lifestyle that helps to build trust.

Michelle, a 39-year-old single parent, is begging for real church, but is very hesitant to return to church as she knows it. You might agree with her sentiment: "I have enough drama in my daily life; why do I want to go to a place that's nothing but drama that no one wants to deal with. That's a waste of time for me. Church is a place where I am supposed to get help, but I get more help watching my preachers on television. I think I'll stick with that."

As I continue to pastor, I have less and less time for drama. In fact, I told my congregation not long ago that I refuse to pastor a drama-filled church. When I said that to the folks, they laughed at me. I then said to them, "We all have issues, but that doesn't mean we have to live in drama. As mature Christians we deal with our issues, but insist that we not live in drama or tolerate others pulling us into drama."

Drama is the opposite of transparency and is an obstacle to trust. Michelle really wants relationships she can trust, but she has been so deeply impacted by her own drama and the drama of the church that she has all but given up trying. So instead, she has detached herself to the extent that her pastor is someone with whom she will never form a real, authentic, transparent relationship. She keeps those who would seek to help her at bay with an assortment of defense mechanisms.

I continue to try to encourage all of the Michelles and Michaels that I meet to reengage with the church by engaging with me in a real, authentic relationship. The investment of time, transparency and trust will determine how this story ends.

But trusting requires vulnerability. We have to become open to hurt and open to healing. God works through people who love Him, people who've hurt and been hurt and people who have been healed and possess the desire to heal. At the same time, we have to become people who are willing to tell our stories of how we hurt and were hurt. That is what transparency is all about. When I'm transparent, I have nothing to hide. When I am transparent I lose or relinquish my shame. It is why Apostle Paul could say (to the Romans/Philippians) I am not ashamed of the Gospel of Jesus Christ because it is the power of God for salvation to all who believe. It is why Jesus, himself, said if you're ashamed of Me, I'll be ashamed of you. Jesus, himself, was seeking transparency.

By the time we find Peter and John in the text of *Acts 3,* they had become vulnerable and transparent. In their three-year walk with Jesus, they'd been hurt before and they'd inflicted hurt before. Yet they'd been healed and were now in a position to heal. For us to get help at some point we are going to have to reach a point of vulnerability and transparency where we can trust these people of God, even when trusting is very hard to do.

Some of the most vulnerable persons in our society are children. Jesus said: "I assure you, unless you turn from your sins and become as little children, you will never get into the Kingdom of Heaven."[2] The humility and transparency of a child is important to emulate. Recently I was really moved and taught by an 8-year-old boy. Brian came up to me after worship with tears in his eyes, holding his little sister's hand. He thanked me for giving him hope. One of the sermon illustrations I used talked about how God can bring divided families back together again. He said his parents (who I know) have been arguing badly and that it really hurts him. His tears demonstrated this reality. I gave him and his sister a big hug and told them I've experienced what they have and that, with God's help, they can overcome. Brian personifies the type of humility, transparency and trust it takes to position oneself for transformation.

> God works through people who love Him, people who've hurt and been hurt and people who have been healed and possess the desire to heal.

Even as we talk about the foundational requirement of trust, I would never suggest that trust be given without discernment. You may be wondering how I can tell who on the path will heal me versus hurt me. You can trust in somebody if:

1. They are pointing to the power of Jesus ("Silver or gold I do not have, but what I have I give you. In the name of Jesus Christ of Nazareth, walk."); and

2. Their motives are for your well-being and not their own (Peter and Paul gained nothing personally—and lost some time worshiping—by helping the beggar); and

3. Their help has no strings attached (they didn't require anything of the beggar except trust).

You may be thinking that this short list severely limits the pool of people who can be trusted. Yet, God still has people positioned for us to trust so that we can get the healing we need.

> Jesus is the man God sent in His own image into the world to show us how to live, how to sacrifice, how to rise above any obstacle thrown in our path

The reason why more than 60% of people today are unchurched or haven't made a faith decision is that they either don't trust God, they don't trust the church and/or they do not trust people; as a result, they are lame and unable to move. Stuck in a condition of begging for the very things that God stands ready to provide, if they will only trust.

One might argue that the beggar was desperate. But even in desperation there must be a level of trust. Do you trust God enough to allow God to lift you right now? Do you trust some people who have been begging to help you to offer you assistance right now? Will you risk trusting Jesus so that you can exchange your begging for a blessing?

Jesus can be trusted.

You may be wondering, who is this Jesus that transforms begging into blessing? People have many images about who Jesus is. We can look through many art books and go to various museums and see that for some Jesus is white, clean, manicured and well groomed. We can go to the movies and can see Him roughed up, beat up, bloody and even crucified. For me, Jesus is a person of color. When I read the Bible that is the image I get. However, I believe people need to see Jesus in their own respective images and then be willing to go beyond the image. Imagine my surprise when seeing all of these pictures of a white Jesus plastered across the walls of Emory United Methodist Church, a predominantly black multicultural church in Washington, DC. Pictures can say a thousand words. Images hold great meaning in people's lives. And these pictures in this church were doing that and more. So I systematically and discretely, over the course of several months, took these pictures off the wall.

However, Jesus is more than a picture, and much deeper than a two-dimensional image.

Jesus is the man God sent in His own image into the world to show us how to live, how to sacrifice, how to rise above any obstacle thrown in our path—even death.

Who is this Jesus?

- He is the man who finds us at our lowest moments and offers us yet another chance.
- He is the man who visits us in our deepest despair and elevates us to see another way.
- He is the man who stumbles upon us in the midst of a crazy guilt trip.
- He forgives us, restores us and sets us on a healthy path again.

Yes, Jesus is far more than pictures and images. Jesus is God himself, wrapped in fleshly garments. He knows how to love us when no other love can be found.

Do you know this Jesus?

- He is Friend to the criminal who wishes to have a clean start.
- He is Comforter to the grieving soul after the third death in three weeks.
- He is the Provider for those who have lost their jobs in the recession.
- He is the Path of Peace amidst political, social and economic unrest.

Jesus is the one who finds us when we are lost, extends favor when we don't deserve it, withholds judgment when we do deserve it and somehow loves us, in spite of us.

Jesus is the answer for the beggar. The criminal justice system punishes when laws are broken. Society condemns when the opportunity to blame is placed before us. The world looks for its own way out when it finds itself in trouble. But Jesus, the beggar's friend, is always there in good times and bad - in sad times and glad.

- He loves us in the pit of the prison cell.
- He loves us in the isolation of ICU.
- He cares for us when we've gone crazy and lost our minds.
- He is the glue when life's tragedies and hardships (lost jobs, lost loves and shattered dreams) break us into pieces.

When we form relationship with Him, suddenly we discover that our begging can be changed to blessing.

This is more than going to church on Sunday. It is more than joining the membership of any church. This is even more than going through the rituals of baptism or the Lord's Supper. Leaving the begging state and traveling along a blessed state happens when, in spite of all the noise and distractions and obstacles that would influence me to do otherwise, I reach out my hand and place it in that Hand of Hope, of Possibility, of Opportunity, of Greatness.

> Our begging can be changed to blessing.

It is a wonderful thing to know that God provides us with a friend who doesn't care about our past, but who is intimately concerned about our present and who holds the plans for our future. That's who Jesus is. And when we get to know Him our lives will be changed forever.

Jesus can be trusted.

You might say that I talk about Jesus as if He is alive. He is and He wants you to know He is. When the women went to anoint Jesus after His death and burial, they encountered an empty tomb. Amazed and alarmed, two men in dazzling robes asked them, "Why do you look for the living among the dead?"[3] We can imagine them asking in fear and panic, "Where is He?" The angels responded, "Do not be afraid, for I know that you are looking for Jesus, who was crucified. He is not here; He has risen, just as He said....Go quickly and tell His disciples: 'He has risen from the dead and is going ahead of you into Galilee. There you will see Him.'"[4]

Galilee was considered a strange and foreign place, where no self-respecting Jew would go. At the time of Jesus' death, it was a physical place that represented a particularly nonreligious place. Today we understand that in the "Galilee" of our time we will find the Risen Christ with the poor, the outcast, the hungry, the rich, the broken-hearted, the lost, the seeking, the prisoner, the orphan, the widowed, the hurt, the self-satisfied.

In "Galilee," the beggar finds hope. In that place there is no democrat or republican, no liberal or conservative politics. In that place no one is concerned about a green party or an independent vote. In that place terrorists and traders must trust Jesus, just as greedy corporate barons and Wall Street gangsters must do. It is in that place where God shows no partiality. That place where the least, the last and the lost, the disturbed, depressed and disenfranchised find someone who is singularly focused on the well-being of their souls and the souls of all. So much so that He died, but then rose to help them.

Yes, Jesus can be trusted. Is trust a four-letter word you can utter now?

Hope

Time to Be REAL
(Relevant, Enthusiastic, Authentic and Loving)

1 What would it take for you to trust God enough to allow Jesus to lift you right now?

2 Identify five people who you suspect might be able to help you... in the name of Jesus.

3 Meet one of them for lunch or coffee with the purpose of discerning whether or not they are trustworthy:

☐ They are pointing to the power of Jesus ("silver and gold have I not. In the name of Jesus, rise"); and

☐ Their motives are for your well-being and not their own (Peter and Paul gained nothing personally—and lost some time worshiping—by helping the beggar); and

☐ Their help has no strings attached (Peter and Paul didn't require anything of the beggar except trust).

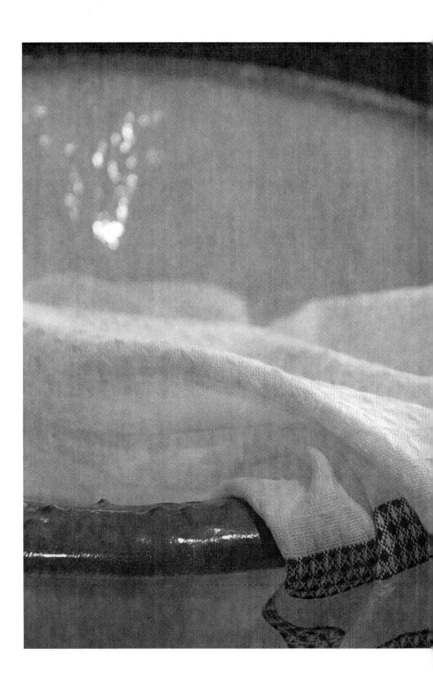

Part 2

Meaningful Engagement

In Part 1 you got a glimpse of what it means to have an authentic encounter, an experience of the God of wholeness. The next step of the path is an important part of the courtship: meaningful engagement.

> **mean·ing·ful** \mē′nǐng-fəl\ **1a.** having a meaning or purpose **b.** full of meaning : significant

This stage in the journey has to involve something significant for you or it will not lead to any place of importance. If it isn't meaningful, it won't be sustainable. Imagine dating someone but never having a meaningful conversation with him or her about things that are important to you and/or them. What are the chances that that relationship will develop into a sustainable, healthy marriage?

> **en·gage·ment** \in-'gāj-mənt, en-\ **1a.** an arrangement to meet or be present at a specified time and place <a dinner *engagement*>
> **2.** something that engages : pledge **3a.** the act of engaging : the state of being engaged **b.** emotional involvement or commitment **c.** betrothal **4.** the state of being in gear

The chapters that follow seek to get you in gear. To get you committed to create an intimate and obedient relationship with Jesus Christ and to enter into more transparent relationships with other believers. To evoke some sort of meaningful emotional connection to God as revealed in Jesus.

The cornerstones of meaningful engagement are: accepting grace, waiting on God and seeking restoration. The significance and impact of these are exponentially increased in a community, specifically a real church.

to bind to oneself as by a pledge
to attract and hold, to cause to
participate, to connect or interlock with
to cause to mesh.

Chapter 5
Awakening to Grace

Show me a real church and I'll show you a church that extends grace in the name of Jesus to all, and receives grace in the name of Jesus from all. Show me a real church and I'll show you a people who know they have a friend in God, and want you to know that because of God's grace, you have a friend in God, too.

Peter and John extended grace, God's unmerited love and favor, to the beggar in *Acts 3*. When the beggar received it, his life was never the same again. Now healed, the beggar suddenly awakened to the fact that he was a friend of God, positioned to develop a deep and abiding friendship with the Christ of his healing. The beggar wanted this so badly that he held on to those representing the Christ—Peter and John—and wouldn't let go.

I believe a whole host of people are begging for a deep and abiding friendship with God. When we awaken to His grace, we will discover that it's been there waiting for us all along.

The Gospel writer Luke, as a physician, made it clear in his writings that it is Jesus' desire to heal you and me from any hopeless situation. He also makes it clear that by the grace of God, the Lord also desires us to be His friends. This notion of "friend of God" was so important that Luke begins the book of *Acts* by calling his audience Theophilus.

"Who is Theophilus?" you ask. Well, when you break this Greek name down, "Theo" means "God;" "Phil" refers to "brother or sister or friend;" and "Us" is the preposition "of." Theophilus means a "friend of God." There's a popular song sung in many churches over the past couple of years by a group known as "Israel and New Breed." The song is entitled, "Friend of God." Many, like those in our fellowship, have sung the lyrics with great power. It goes, "I am a friend of God. I am a friend of God. I am a friend of God. He calls me friend." The reference is to Theophilus, a friend of God. A real church is filled with people who know they have a friend in God. But a real church also yearns for people to experience God as a friend.

And so Luke sets out in his two books of the Bible, *Luke* and *Acts*, to extend a healing hand to reach God's friends. To do that, he makes the understanding of Theophilus clear. While a lot of people believe that Theophilus was a person, nobody knows who Theophilus really was. All we know him to be is a friend of God. That means God is talking to the people of The Way—Christians. But he is also talking to people who do not yet know The Way because God through Jesus Christ loves these individuals, too. He makes it clear that God loves those who have awakened to Him. But God also loves those who have yet to experience His love. While many of us may feel that we're not friends yet, Jesus views us as friends and even sacrificed His life so that we might know that we are His friends. When I awakened to grace, by His grace, I figured this out.

How do people awaken to grace? I believe one key way is letting people know that Jesus offers a second chance, like the beggar found out. A real church offers people a second, third, fourth and even a four hundredth chance for a friendship with God. A real church knows that Jesus will continue offering all of these chances to stumbling believers today. There are many people who are frustrated with church and have left the church—multitudes of people who don't feel that church really matters—even more who are disenfranchised with the church because feelings of guilt and failure have caused them to believe that they have no chance of being a friend of God.

I remember preaching my Uncle Pete's funeral in April of 2008. You probably have somebody like my Uncle Pete in your family. Maybe you are my Uncle Pete. My Uncle Pete was someone who believed in God, but did not go to church. His life often reflected the love of God, but then there were sides of him that made you scratch your head and wonder if he'd really met Jesus.

I preached Pete's eulogy from the parable of the lost son in *Luke 15*. I began by saying a certain man had two sons. If you know the story, then you know that one son became lost, while one stayed home. But the fact of the matter was that God loved both of them and considered them friends. Both were his sons and both were challenged to awaken to God's grace. The son everybody thought was lost forever, eventually awakened to the fact that God really loved him. That was my Uncle Pete. With all of the trails of mess in his life, he had awakened to the fact that God did really love him. His faith journey simply had not brought him to the church house for regular worship yet!

How do people awaken to grace?

A lot of folks can relate to Uncle Pete. After the funeral service, one of my cousins came up to me and said, "Oh thank you, Joey. You don't know what you did today." I said, "You're welcome but what do you mean?" He said, "There were a lot of people in this church who felt like they had lost all of their chances at heaven. But because they heard that God still loves them and wants to be in relationship with them, you let them know that God wasn't finished with them yet."

Depending upon your unique story you might be a person of The Way or not yet a person of The Way. No matter your circumstance, because of His grace extended to you, God is your friend. Many of us have friends, family, associations and strangers we need to talk to, who do not know the Lord, but who are still friends of God. Many of us need to share with others the stories of what the goodness of the Lord has meant to our lives—others who have yet to believe in God, but by grace, are still friends of God.

That's why every time you and I greet someone, we've got to be aware that we are speaking to a friend of God. Luke is talking to

Theophilus, the Friend of God, a person who cannot be defined, cannot be identified, but a person who is still the creation of God. Jesus is trying to reach everybody. Why? Because it's His desire to see us healed. Healed from begging for a real life, awakened to His grace!

You might wonder what it looks and feels like to be awakened to His grace. One of my former pastors, Carey E. Pointer, Sr., gave me my initial opportunities to preach, and was the pastor who licensed me and oversaw my ordination in the Baptist church. Those three years for me in the Baptist church were a real education, both positive and negative. However, I'll never forget Rev. Pointer telling me one day about when he was a young popular preacher in the countryside of Northern Virginia. He had gotten to a point of burnout. He was in the process of interviewing for churches hoping that one would call him to be their pastor. But all the while he was facing burnout. One week he was called by the deacon of a church and invited to come preach at that church the following Sunday. He went there so burned out that he had no sermon prepared. When it was time for him to preach, he stood up and, with tears streaming down his face, admitted to the congregation that he had nothing. He sang a song, pronounced the benediction and ran home in fear. Fear for his future, fear for his career and fear that he might never get the opportunity to preach again.

> Grace represents
>
> God's favor

Feeling like a failure, Rev. Pointer was hesitant to answer the phone that night when it rang. It was the deacon of the church. "Reverend, we want you to preach next Sunday." Rev. Pointer couldn't understand why they would even ask him to come back, but he went back the next Sunday. Still burned out and with nothing, Rev. Pointer stood to preach the non-existent sermon. As he began to open his mouth, a woman stood up and shouted:

Reverend, excuse me, I don't mean to interrupt service, but I just have to share one thing. I came to church last Sunday prepared to commit suicide. I said I'd give God one last chance to speak to me as to why I shouldn't, but my plan was to come to church, leave and take my life. I was prepared to do it, but it was the song you sang last Sunday that caused me to change my mind and to see that God had far more for my life that I had ever seen. Before you preach today, I just wanted to stand up and say, thank you.

Needless to say the entire church, including Rev. Pointer, was never the same again.

Within Rev. Pointer's story, there are many forms of grace. In fact, if you are really going to understand this grace thing, then you've got to realize that grace often works in stages. First you've got to get to the point where you are willing to start walking with Jesus, learning the ways of His life. You get to that point by hanging out with people and in places His word is being taught and His ways lifted up. Fifteen years ago, my cousin Neal called me up on the phone, inquiring about a life change. Neal asked me why it was that I seemed to be so blessed, so happy. He said he'd been watching me for years, and the blessings and the happiness surrounding me were so strong that he wanted what I had. I told him flat out that he needed to start walking with Jesus. He asked, "How do I do that?" I told him, "Number one, let's you and me stay connected and keep these conversations going." I then said to him, "Number two, take your behind to a good church where the word is being preached so that you can learn and grow." Neal started the journey. Perhaps you need to start the journey.

Then you've got to decide that you want to follow Him. A disciple is a learner and follower of Jesus Christ—somebody who's made up their mind to pursue a deep and abiding friendship with Jesus because they've awakened to the grace of God in their lives. What stage are you on? You see, there are those who are just hanging around a little bit, and that's all right. If you hang around looking for Jesus long enough, Jesus is going to find you. That's what happened to Neal. We kept talking about Jesus and the words we shared long distance over the phone were being confirmed by the Word preached at church and experienced in his everyday life. Once Neal decided to start walking with Jesus, learning about Him and following His ways, his three-year unemployment period came to an end. Once Neal started going to a real church, his fractured family started

making moves to come back together again. Once Neal saw that Jesus
was real in his life, he couldn't let go of Him. Once you hang around
Jesus long enough, and you see that Jesus is for real, you awaken to grace.
That's when you start the path that church folk call discipleship.

Grace represents God's favor, His undeserved love. It is the good
stuff that happens, not due to anything you or I have done, but because
of what God did through the saving love of His son Jesus. Why?
Because God calls you friend and God loves you.

John Wesley, the founder of Methodism, spent a lot of time
explaining to folks the importance of grace. He did so because he
realized that we can try all we want at some things, but unless God
touches us, it doesn't happen. He talked about four kinds of grace that
serve four distinct roles:

1. Grace looks out for me when I don't know I'm being looked
    out for. It's God's grace that watches over me when I'm
    sleeping.
2. Grace puts me back in line when I'm out of line; wipes the slate
    clean when I've messed up.
3. Grace sets me apart to do God's will.
4. Grace places me to be exactly where I'm meant to be, to play
    my role in the body of Christ.

Fifteen years later, my cousin Neal is experiencing each of these
kinds of grace. He can now see how God was watching over him when
he didn't even know it—prevenient grace. A gun shot wound that
almost paralyzed him, episodes where jail could have snatched him and
many other life events that could have taken him away from us fuel his
understanding of prevenient grace.

He can see how the Lord used our conversations over the phone
and over the miles to get his life back in line with the Lord's purposes
for his life—justifying grace. When he thinks about the mess in his life
and that Jesus has forgiven him of all of it, joy overwhelms him.

When Neal and I talk about this, I think of the Etch-A-Sketch
board I used to play with as a kid. You know, the red paneled drawing
toy with two knobs and a screen. By turning the knobs you controlled
an invisible pen that drew straight lines and crooked lines on the screen.
You could draw things all you wanted. Oftentimes in my drawing, I'd

make a mess. But the wonderful thing about Etch-a-Sketch was that if it didn't turn out the way you wanted it to, all you have to do is shake it to start over with a clean screen. The Etch-A-Sketch design is like justifying grace. No matter how much we mess up, God can shake us right back to alignment with Him.

Over these 15 years of journeying with Jesus, Neal has now found himself set apart to help churches build churches. He is watching how God is using him and his entrepreneurial gifts to bless people and expand the church's capacity to reach people. He's living out his call, set apart to serve the Lord in this capacity—sanctifying grace.

As I reflect on how God used many ways to speak to me and move me toward pastoral ministry, I have noticed ever since I was a little kid that I was always at the end of the table. I was never in the middle of the table; I was never in the center of the group. I was always on the edge—always set apart.

> We can try all we want at some things, but unless God touches us, it doesn't happen.

Set apart to serve—usually entails a series of events and "coincidences" that put you exactly where God wants you to be. God has a reason, a season, a plan and a purpose for each one of you. He's not going to leave you alone, He's not going to leave you empty, He's not going to leave you hanging until He finishes what He started in you. And so He sets you apart, and you may not be yet where you think you ought to be, but guess what? It's all a part of His plan. You may have fallen off the road, rolled down the hill and wondered whether or not God loves you.

Yes, God still loves you; He's just bringing you along as part of His plan. He's setting you apart in order for you to be different. Setting you apart in order for you to be able to fulfill the things of God, not only in your life, but also in the lives of those who have your name written on their foreheads. He's setting you apart in order to have favor with those who need to know Him.

And through Neal's moves from Pittsburgh, Pennsylvania to Columbus, Ohio to Oakland, California, he is watching God place him and line him up where God wants him to be for God's purposes and plans—perfecting grace. Three churches and multitudes of people have already been blessed by his building talents, all because Neal has been exactly where God wants him to be.

That's what perfecting grace is all about. God lining you up perfectly in His will. Do you know that you can be imperfect, but perfect? Do you know you can be imperfect; you can have flaws, but still be perfect? I went to get some jeans the other day and the jeans fit me, and I said, "Praise the Lord!" And I've been wearing them for the last couple of weeks.

I washed them the other day and I looked inside and they said, "Irregular." I said, "Lord have mercy!" I bought some irregular jeans and the tag didn't say "Irregular" on the front, but when I looked inside the pants, it did. I started looking for where the irregularities of the pants were, and I just couldn't find them. It's because those pants were right for me, even though they may have not been right for somebody else.

Although there were some imperfections that I can't recognize, in God's plan they are perfect. Don't you know that God has a will and plan for you, and as long as you walk in it, you're going to be all right? You might not be fully physically well. You might have some issues, but as long as you're walking in His will—in His perfect will—that Perfecting Grace will keep you, that Perfecting Grace will bless you, that Perfecting Grace will shower blessings upon you.

Neal has never lived with the kind of peace that he's living with now. Does he still have troubles? Yes. Do crises still occur in his life? Yes. Do the challenges of life worry and disturb him? Yes. Just like all of us. But because he has awakened to grace, he now lives with the confidence that through this meaningful engagement with God, God will take care of him and all who God loves. Neal is a friend of God.

Do you wish to be God's friend today? Just tell him "Yes" and start the journey!

Time to Be REAL
(Relevant, Enthusiastic, Authentic and Loving)

❶ What would be different if you really believed that you were a friend of God; that God was a good friend of yours?

❷ Where have you seen grace active in your life?

❸ Pay attention to grace this week. Make note of situations that make you aware of the amazing grace that God is surrounding you and your loved ones with.

Chapter 6
Waiting for God

Show me a real church and I'll show you a church that waits for a movement of God. Show me a real church and I will show you a people heavily engaged in prayer.

The beggar in *Acts 3* had to wait a long time for his healing, but in his waiting he experienced the movement of God. The disciples praying for the power of the Holy Ghost to heal in *Acts 1* had to wait for it as a part of Jesus' command. But in their waiting, they prayed and discovered that when God makes a promise, God does not disappoint. Waiting and praying are critical cornerstones of a real church.

Prayer is simply communication with God that summons His presence in heaven to become real on earth. Prayer is the medium through which we fellowship with God and get our daily marching orders from God for every aspect of our lives. Prayer is the silent yet verbal conversation that God has with us and that we have with God which allows God to encourage us, to comfort us, to counsel us, to rebuke us and even to correct us. Prayer is that sharing time with God where God can speak clearly God's will for our lives. Some people interact with God best on their knees, with heads bowed and eyes closed. Some do it best by walking around with open eyes. Some people resonate with God best in prayer in total silence; some by listening to music that relaxes their soul. However you can best hear from the Lord in these waiting moments; that's the posture you want to adopt.

More and more I am becoming an advocate of Howard Thurman's approach to prayer. Thurman was a great mystic, theologian and preacher of the 20th century. Thurman believed that 80% of prayer is listening, and the other 20% is talking. He advanced that if we are looking to hear from God or communicate with God in our waiting moments, we shouldn't be doing much talking. How can you hear from God if you are doing all the talking? Have you been listening for God? Real churches with real people wait for a move of God, a wait that is heavily grounded in prayer.

> When we listen for God, we need to see God, to hear God and to feel God.

A good friend of my father's, when I was a teenager, was a man by the name of Edwin Nichols. Dr. Nichols, by trade and training, is an industrial psychologist trained in understanding the behaviors, attitudes, norms and mores of the various races, cultures and ethnicities of the world. Dr. Nichols likes to describe and define "listening" by looking at the word the Chinese use for listening. Our Western understanding of listening is defined in terms of hearing and seeing, he told me once. But when you look at the Chinese "word" for listening, you'll notice that it is comprised of three symbols: the symbol for seeing, the symbol for hearing and the symbol for feeling. And so when we listen for God, we need to see God, to hear God and to feel God.

There are many different types of prayer but two general movements in our prayers: outgoing and incoming; talking and listening. There is a role for each. The prayers typically heard in local church settings are "outgoing" (*e.g.*, petition and intercession). And these prayers are crucial to the body of Christ. Petitions and intercessions have saved many a life and many a family, and caused a multitude of closed doors to open and countless lives to be healed!!

I remember a church in southeast Washington, D.C. that intentionally prayed every Friday night for the return of one of their young members, who had lost her way and gotten messed up in the crack cocaine epidemic of the late 1980's and early 1990's. Every Friday and even at other times, they offered petition and intercession to God, asking God to return their loved one as the Gospel of Mark describes, "clothed and in their right mind." For weeks, they waited and prayed, waited and prayed, waited and prayed. Then, one Friday night, while they were praying, the woman walked into the prayer meeting, clothed and in her right mind. Holy Ghost pandemonium took over the sanctuary. After many hugs and kisses and moments of rejoicing, the woman who'd been lost began testifying about her being "out there." But then she said in a moment of recovery, seeking to turn her life around, "I kept hearing and seeing these people in my mind praying for me. And I realized I had to get back to the place where they are praying. I am back, and the Lord has healed me!"

The Bible has a lot to say about this kind of "outgoing" prayer:

> "You do not have because you do not ask." James 4:2

> "This is the confidence we have before Him, that, if we ask anything according to His will, He hears us." 1 John 5:14

> "Again I say to you, that if two of you agree on earth about anything that they may ask, it shall be done for them by My Father who is in heaven. For where two or three have gathered in My name, I am there in their midst." Matthew 18:19-20

Additionally the Bible has a lot to show us about the importance of incoming prayer as well. When it comes to seeking guidance and leading from God, we must retreat from our surroundings and become quiet.

The disciples needed that in the Upper Room. They gathered—men and women—together and prayed.[5] While we weren't told exactly how they prayed, we can surmise that they talked to God, listened for God individually and through one another.

Jesus, himself, made it a regular practice to retreat and escape to a quiet place to pray. And He encouraged His disciples to do the same.

Jesus got up early in the morning to find a quiet place, a place that was isolated and secluded, where it was just him and God and elements of creation around him. Jesus was so isolated in prayer that the Gospel writers would report that people would have to go find him. We need to be able to get away like that with God and God alone.

I know people who even today practice getting away to a quiet place to pray.

Juanita Rasmus serves at St. John's Downtown in Houston, Texas with her husband—and one of my prayer partners—Rudy Rasmus. Juanita often goes for week-long silent retreats where she doesn't talk at all. She spends the entire week listening for God and returns from these retreats refreshed, renewed and revived with a clear word from the Lord.

Gary Henderson, another of my prayer partners, will from time to time escape to a monastery and assume the place and posture of a monk for a period of time, to be silent and listen for God.

I used to be an avid road biker. I would regularly ride 10, 15, 20, sometimes 50 miles on a road bike when I'd go out. My bike riding time, through forests and parks, country roads and along creeks and rivers, used to be part of my prayer time because it was just God and me alone, communing in nature. I used to see and hear things I would never see or hear in any other place that allowed me to get in touch with God in ways that I couldn't otherwise.

Whenever possible, I like to escape to the beach. Just feeling the breeze and listening to the roar of the ocean and the sea gulls chirping and watching how the sun, the moon, the water, the sand and all living creation around it react, places me in a mood and posture where I can fully surrender to God and can hear God in my waiting moments, and I gain even greater strength to wait on God to move.

We need to listen for God through music, through people, through nature, through events and through circumstances that take place in our lives.

When I was seeking to discern in 1990 and 1991 whether God wanted me to leave my full time job and get into ministry full-time, I was fully engaged in seeking to hear, see and feel God's will. I spent a year in prayer and discernment. As a part of this, I went to a week long revival in Gary, Indiana[6], talked to friends and mentors and just listened to them, went for walks in quiet places and to the beach to gain direction. Believe it or not, I have found that one of the greatest places of prayer is in the shower, particularly if everyone else in my house is already gone and I can use up all the hot water for myself!! Usually when I hit the shower, God speaks.

We have to find places where we position ourselves to hear God speak. The disciples had to do that. At the beginning of *Acts 1,* we see the disciples locked up in fear following Jesus' resurrection and ascension. They were lost during that time so they were trying to find a quiet place where they could hear from Him, where they could wait for the timing of God, for the movement of the Holy Spirit.[7]

A lot of people who beg are in that same situation. We beg because we're lost. We need to hear a word, a direction. We need God to be clear with us as He was with Isaiah. You will turn to your right and turn to your left, and then you will hear God say, this is the way, walk in it. We need to hear a word when we are lost in the wildernesses of life.

The wilderness can be a great place for prayer—for listening for God—for it is in the wildernesses of life that God has our attention. It is in the wildernesses of life where God speaks some of His greatest revelations that are life-transforming.

> We have to find places where we position ourselves to hear God speak.

Some of my most recent life-transforming experiences have happened in the desert. For two years in a row, I took week long vacations in Palm Desert, CA, where in August the temperature is 90 degrees at its coolest point of the day and 115 during the hottest.

I will never forget my experience at the Joshua Tree National Park there, right outside of Palm Desert. Outside of it being hot as hell, there was very little evidence of life with the exception of the Joshua tree. It is the tree that literally gives every other living thing what it needs to survive in the desert. Every plant, animal and insect gets its water from the Joshua tree. The tree isn't all that impressive. It looks like it's in the cactus family. It is not more than 3–4 feet high. Yet it captures and stores water from the two or three big downpours the desert receives over the course of a year, and for the rest of that year—even in the most barren, driest places—it supplies life. If there is no Joshua tree in this desert, there is no life.

The name "Joshua" is the root of the word from which we get "Jesus." It means "salvation." It is in the desert that we find salvation. Prayer is likewise life giving for the beggar who is in the wilderness. Prayer is how we tap into endless streams of living water, the water that heals and restores us. Prayer is where the communication and personal understanding of salvation happens. God speaks to us in our deserts and wildernesses, and saves us. It is in that wilderness of life that God speaks a word of deliverance, of hope. Everybody needs a Joshua tree in our desert moments!

> God, more than anything, searches for the yearning of the heart.

Hopefully you understand that prayer is more than the regiment we see on Sunday morning or by televangelists. God is not concerned with how eloquent our prayers are or how flowery our words are. God, more than anything, searches for the yearning of the heart. The longing like the deer pants for water.[8] God is more concerned with our desire to be present with Him so that He might speak, than about the words we might utter.

Paul tells us to pray unceasingly, which means that we need to pray whenever we are moved to pray. Whether it is outgoing and public, or whether it is to sneak away for a quiet moment of listening for God. Some people pray in bathroom stalls at work. Others step outside for a walk down the street. Others run a short errand.

The church that practices this kind of prayer in real, powerful and authentic ways finds God moving in its midst and on its behalf in ways that other methods could not produce. When we practice and participate in prayer like this, tumors shrink in the name of Jesus, cancer disappears in the name of Jesus, broken families come back together again in the name of Jesus and money is found even during recession times in the name of Jesus. People down and out bounce back up in the name of Jesus. Jobs are found where there are no jobs. Opportunity is discovered where every door before was shut.

Real churches develop the spiritual discipline of prayer. We are intentional about gathering people for times of petitioning and of listening (seeing, hearing, feeling). Prayer becomes an intentional and integral part of the weekly life of the church. You see it and feel it in worship, in small groups, in meetings, in classes and in other gatherings. The real church realizes it needs to be led by the hand and voice of God, and acts out of that understanding.

At Emory, we seek to be intentional about prayer by, amongst many things, having a Sabbath day of prayer at church. Several years ago, we had a prayer weekend, where we invited a colleague of mine, Dennis Blackwell, to lead us. Dennis, a great pastor from Camden, NJ, did a workshop on prayer and preached on Sunday morning. He taught us that just as we take a Sabbath day for God, the church needs to have a Sabbath day to refrain from the normal workings of church (*e.g.,* meetings) and that that day should be set aside as a day of prayer within the normal operations. So, at Emory we've made Wednesday our Sabbath day of prayer. We have daytime prayer from noon–1 and we have evening prayer at 7:07.

> When we gather and intentionally listen for God, beggars find that great things can happen.

We do that to have a designated time for us to specifically engage in talking to God and listening for God so that we, as a congregation, can get direction from God. When two or three are gathered, real church is taking place. When we gather and intentionally listen for God, beggars find that great things can happen. We can get through the waiting and be thrust into blessing.

Time to Be REAL
(Relevant, Enthusiastic, Authentic and Loving)

1 Listen for God with your eyes, your ears, your spirit and your body. What is God seeking to tell you through music, through people, through nature, through events and through circumstances that are taking place in your life?

2 What "impossible" thing do you want to ask God for?

3 In the coming week, identify a quiet place that you will go to hear God speak. What do you need to do to continue the practice of quiet prayer?

Read

Chapter 7
Experiencing Restoration

Show me a real church and I'll show you a church that seeks to restore its people and community in the name of Jesus. Show me a real church and I'll show you a people who are active in working with God to restore somebody.

Surrounding the time of Jesus' trial, crucifixion, death and resurrection, we find Peter and the disciples forsaking Jesus and fleeing the scene. They were so filled with fear that they forgot most of what Jesus had told them. They failed Jesus, failed each other, and failed to fully understand the resurrection. Then they returned to something they used to be good at: fishing.

And now, as *John 21* portrays, even after encountering the Risen Christ twice, they were even failing at fishing; what they loved to do and used to make their livelihood doing. These experienced fishermen were in their boat, casting their large net on the water for hours without evidence of a single fish in the sea. After fishing for hours and catching nothing, Jesus told them to throw the nets over the opposite side of the same boat in the same sea. He didn't direct them to a different location. He didn't have them use a different technique. This slight change in direction—going to the opposite side of the boat—yielded a net so full of fish that the net and boat could barely hold them.

After struggling to lift a net brimming with 153 fish into their boat, Jesus then calls the fishermen onshore for breakfast. So Peter and the others prepare to eat the catch of the day with Jesus. Come and dine, the Lord implores them. Then after the meal, something happens:

> *When they had finished eating, Jesus said to Simon Peter, "Simon son of John, do you truly love me more than these?"*
>
> *"Yes, Lord," he said, "You know that I love you."*
>
> *Jesus said, "Feed my lambs."*
>
> *Again Jesus said, "Simon son of John, do you truly love me?"*
>
> *He answered, "Yes, Lord, you know that I love you."*
>
> *Jesus said, "Take care of my sheep."*
>
> *The third time He said to him, "Simon son of John, do you love me?" Peter was hurt because Jesus asked him the third time, "Do you love me?"*
>
> *He said, "Lord, you know all things; you know that I love you."*
>
> *Jesus said, "Feed my sheep...Follow me!"⁹*

Peter in his brokenness of denying the Christ, in his pain of forsaking his Lord and fleeing, and in his guilt of rejecting the work that Jesus had for him and the others to do, now finds Jesus a third time after the resurrection. In this third encounter Jesus restores Peter so He can recommission him. This restoration was initiated by Jesus, orchestrated by Jesus and perfected by Jesus. Do you need to be restored today? Do you need to restore somebody? Real churches restore and are restored on a daily basis.

The Old Testament is filled with detailed stories of the deadly sins in action: lust, gluttony, greed, sloth, wrath, envy and pride. These wrongdoings and transgressions often leave us in a chasm of guilt, shame, frustration and pain, begging for another chance or a new life. But the wonderful thing about Jesus is that after the mess and in the midst of our pain, Jesus shows up to restore. Wow! In the words of Stephanie Mills, a popular R&B soloist in the 70s–80s, "I Never Knew Love Like This Before." In most cases, after people sin, God restores. I'm a witness that Jesus is the beggar's pain medication.

This divine restoration process is rooted in the salvation that God offers to all. Salvation in its simplest form comes from the Greek word "sozo," which means "to be healed; to be made complete; to be made whole." Many people think that salvation is strictly a spiritual matter. This notion is enforced by people who ask, "Are you saved?" and only focus on the confession with our mouths and belief in our hearts.[10] I can't tell you how many times people have stopped me on the buses and subways in the DC metro area asking this question. But while the spiritual aspect of salvation is its root, you and me are not complete nor are we whole nor are we saved, unless every aspect of our lives is consistent with the salvation given to us freely by Jesus Christ.

> Salvation in its simplest form comes from the Greek word "sozo," which means "to be healed; to be made complete; to be made whole."

Please understand that this is a life-long process and a daily journey. Our salvation is instantaneous when we accept Jesus as our Lord and personal Savior. We have accepted His promise of salvation and Jesus never breaks a promise. However, our salvation is a continuous event. This is why Apostle Paul later exhorts us to work out our salvation in fear and trembling. Salvation is something to be revered and appreciated and addressed daily. It should not be taken for granted. People think church folk are such hypocrites because we walk around saying we are saved with just a spiritual understanding but don't realize that if I'm saved spiritually but my relationships are jacked up or my finances are a shamble or my emotions are out of control, then I am sending a message that doesn't reflect completeness. Granted, all of us are a work in progress!! None of us are perfect or a finished product yet. God will take care of that in the life to come.

At Emory, we believe that salvation and restoration come as we journey with Jesus, helping people become a visible example of love, leading people to a Christ-centered WHOLEness from Georgia Avenue to across the globe. We want ourselves to be and people to be:

> **W**ell physically
> **H**ealed emotionally
> **O**pened and Obedient to the movement of God's Spirit
> **L**oved unconditionally
> **E**mpowered financially

To us this encompasses completeness in this world.

Well: Throughout the Gospels, Jesus healed people physically, in addition to healing them spiritually. Our bodies are a temple unto God and need appropriate care.

Healed: Critical to Jesus' mission was that people be clothed and in their right minds. Peace of mind is a gift from God and a precious treasure we value.

Open and Obedient: Being open to the movement of God's Spirit is just the first step. Our Lord's desire is for us to walk in relationship with Jesus. As we do so, we are drawn closer to God and closer to one another, and gain wisdom for handling the trials of everyday life.

Loved: Everybody deserves and desires to be loved. Love is the crucial ingredient to Christian character.

Empowered: Jesus viewed money as a tool to accomplish God-given goals. A healthy approach to money grants peace of mind, body and soul. The proper use of money can bless multitudes.

I could tell you story after story of rich and poor, middle class and no class, affluent and needy people who have been broken by life, only to be restored by God to wholeness. I could tell you of broken narratives, coming back together.

I could tell you stories of children getting lost through the temptations of the street or the seduction of the Internet, coming back to their senses and living better lives.

I could tell you stories of people who were in prison or imprisoned behind the bars of their own souls, who are now living productive lives.

I could tell you stories of those who lost their homes and were rendered homeless while still living in a house, who now have a place to live, a solid family and a bright present and future.

I could tell you stories of people who have broken addictions by God's grace and who love people in ways that no words can define because they have witnessed the love of God that has lifted their own lives, love that restores!

After you have failed, in any or all of the areas described above, the Lord wants to do a re-mix on you. Through His grace extended and received, you can emerge closer to the abundant life God has for you. Be restored and restore somebody!

Time to Be REAL
(Relevant, Enthusiastic, Authentic and Loving)

❶ Spend this week listening for what God is getting ready to restore in your life. Pay special attention to encounters you have, to dreams you have, to waking thoughts you have and to impressions you receive during your listening prayer times.

❷ Focus on one area per day. Ask God to reveal to you what needs restoring in each area and write it down.

- Well Physically:
- Healed Emotionally:
- Opened and Obedient to the movement of God's Spirit:
- Loved Unconditionally:
- Empowered Financially:

❸ The last two days of the week seek discernment about which one needs to be restored first. Identify your first simple steps toward restoration and begin walking!

Chapter 8
Celebrating Victory

Show me a real church and I'll show you a church that celebrates people getting up after being knocked down. Show me a real church and I'll show you a people with grateful, joyful hearts.

The central reality of the beggar is that he got knocked down. In fact, he may have been knocked down for his entire life. But the truth was that though he was down, he got up. More specifically, he was released from being lame and restored in the name of Jesus.

> *He jumped to his feet and began to walk. Then he went with them into the temple courts, walking and jumping, and praising God. When all the people saw him walking and praising God, they recognized him as the same man who used to sit begging at the temple gate called Beautiful, and they were filled with wonder and amazement at what had happened to him.*[11]

Real churches celebrate people rising up after falling down. The beggar gets up leaping and praising God!

Several years ago at Emory there was a man called James   a great man with a tremendous sense of humor and a wonderful personality. James loves God and loves the church. In particular, James loved to sing and sang with the choir on a regular basis.

James however constantly fought the pain, discomfort and personal embarrassment of spinal cord degeneration. He was deformed and somewhat crippled because of his condition. These physical challenges often knocked him down, physically and spiritually, but also mentally and emotionally. James was a warrior, but when these challenges knocked him down, they were devastating in nature.

> What we learned in this whole experience was that God could be trusted.

On one occasion, after being knocked down by a back condition that impacted his ability to breathe and talk, James went into the hospital for a simple procedure to help correct some difficulties. Little did he know, however, that he would be in a supreme fight for his life. An unforeseen error in the operating room suddenly landed James in the surgical ICU. For days on end, James was fighting for his life. Our church prayed for him before he went to surgery, during surgery and after surgery. We intensified our prayers both at the hospital and at the church. Our faith in God was stretched to its greatest limits because we had believed God would heal James and now suddenly we were watching James on the brink of death. What we learned in this whole experience was that God could be trusted.

And we learned that even when our faith is reduced to the size of a mustard seed, God still has the power to prevail. What we also discovered is that even when our faith runs out, as for many it did during James's ordeal, God can still be trusted.

Weeks later, God moved. James received a miraculous intervention from God—he emerged from his coma. The seemingly endless numbers of tubes running in and out of his body were removed. And not long after, James returned home.

There was pandemonium at Emory the day he returned to church. James was famous before his ordeal for singing the solo parts of a song entitled "Sovereign…" by Daryl Coley.

> *Who am I, to question His wisdom (I am nothing)?*
> *Who am I, to question God's judgment (I am nothing)?*
> *Who am I, to be offended by His ways?*
> *By word He allows to be*
> *I must realize that my God is (sovereign)*
> *The Lord is (sovereign)*
> *Sovereign (The Lord my God is sovereign)*
> *He is sovereign*
>
> ***Chorus***
> *Sovereign, Sovereign*
> *The Lord my God is Sovereign*
> *He can do whatever He wants to do*
> *He can do whatever He wants to do*
> *When He wants to*
> *God can do whatever He wants to do,*
> *How He wants to*
> *Because He's sovereign,*
> *God is God*

Whenever James would sing this solo part, it would move people to tears. Whenever you looked at James, even before his surgery, you could tell how much he suffered and how much he struggled.

With the little strength he had that Sunday following his deliverance from his coma, he got up and sang "Sovereign." There was bedlam in the sanctuary. Not a dry eye could be found in the place.

James had been knocked down, but he got back up by the grace and power of Jesus Christ. He and his church family celebrated and praised God with our whole beings.

Your story and my story may not be like James's story, but real churches celebrate victories like this large and small.

For example, recently one of our members graduated with a PhD in pharmacology, a tremendous feat to say the least. Her difficulty, however, came when she had to take her licensing examinations to practice her skills in pharmacology. While she excelled in the classroom, the licensing examination knocked her down. On two occasions she took the exam, only to fail. But when she went the third time she prepared a different way. She entered into a month long time of fasting and prayer. And the church prayed with her. When she returned to us and the passing grades came in, we celebrated mightily in worship.

These stories can be celebrated. These stories must be celebrated. Real churches take time in worship, in small groups, in other places and spaces to celebrate victory in the name of Jesus.

It is important to celebrate victory as the beggar did. The writer of the text took the time to point out what to do after being restored. Celebrate! We need to pay attention to it.

> In a world that often celebrates people falling from grace, God wants us to take time to celebrate people rising because of grace.

In a world that often celebrates people falling from grace, God wants us to take time to celebrate people rising because of grace.

We could talk for days about celebrities and political figures falling from grace, and the amount of media and cocktail party attention paid them: Michael Vick and the dog incident, Bill and Monica, Elizabeth Dole calling her political opponent Godless, Britney wrestling with sanity, the prostitute known as "the DC Madam" who ended up committing suicide over her fall. These are the public stories of failure that we are bombarded with on a regular basis. But what about the stories of victory that God brings into our lives because we were faithful enough to trust that in the garbage cans of despair, God's love still shows us grace? And by His grace, His direction, and His ability to restore, victory is possible.

If we don't take the time to celebrate victory, we aren't thanking God. If we don't take the time to celebrate, we aren't sharing the full story of what God can do, has done and might do for someone else. Without taking the time to celebrate the victories, we can give the false impression that God is not really at work in the world. When we don't take time to celebrate our God-given victories, large and small, it will be more difficult for us to be resilient the next time life knocks us down.

An attitude of gratitude cannot be cultivated without celebration. Without gratitude we miss out on a key element of what it means to worship God. We were made to worship God. If you feel like you are missing something, maybe that's it. There is only one way to find out— try it and see what happens.

Time to Be REAL
(Relevant, Enthusiastic, Authentic and Loving)

❶ What is your story of falling down and being picked up by the love and grace of God? How did you celebrate it? If you didn't celebrate it, find a way to do it now. *I was stationed in Ill.*

I decided I wasn't going to church any more until I was sure I was doing it because I wanted to not because I was taught to go.

❷ This week, look for opportunities to celebrate victories at work, at home, at church, on the streets, on the Internet and wherever else you might go.

❸ Go to a church that you know regularly celebrates victories so that you might experience a key part of worship that you may have been missing.

BONUS: If you are currently attending a church that doesn't celebrate victories, talk with your pastor about some ways you think the church could regularly celebrate victories in worship.

Read

Part 3

Radical Expectation

As you saw in Part 2, "Meaningful Engagement" leads to a life change. As our lives change from what we want to what God wants our expectations expand radically.

> **Radical** \'ra-di-kəl\ **1.** of, relating to, or proceeding from a root: d: designed to remove the root of a disease or all diseased and potentially diseased tissue <radical surgery> <radical mastectomy> **2.** of or relating to the origin: fundamental; **3a.** marked by a considerable departure from the usual or traditional: extreme **b.** tending or disposed to make extreme changes in existing views, habits, conditions, or institutions **c.** advocating extreme measures to retain or restore a political state of affairs <the radical right>. Slang: excellent, cool

Jesus was a radical in all senses of the word. He was sent to: a) wash away our sin (root of a disease); b) refocus God's children on the fundamentals ("love the Lord your God with all your heart, soul, mind, strength…and your neighbor as yourself.")[12]; and c) restore a spiritual state by a demonstrating extreme departures from the institutional church (loving the outcasts and challenging the system).

> **Expectation** \'ek-'spek-'tā-shən, ik-\ **1.** the act or state of expecting: anticipation <in expectation of what would happen> **2a.** something expected <not up to expectations> <expectations for an economic recovery> **b.** basis for expecting: assurance <they have every expectation of success> **c.** prospects of inheritance —usually used in plural **3.** the state of being expected **4a.** expectancy 2b **b.** expected value

We know from numerous studies of classroom learning if the expectations are low, then so is the performance. Perhaps many churches that people are actively turning away from are suffering from the syndrome of low expectations.

A real church seeks to cause others to follow in Jesus' footsteps. To find these places and spaces, we must readjust our expectations to match His radical nature. We beggars should expect a church that is authentic, that loves without strings attached, that forgives and accepts folks as they are and that breaks down barriers and builds bridges.

Read

Chapter 9
Real Church is Authentic

S how me a real church and I'll show you a church that is not phony or pretentious. Show me a real church and I'll show you people who come as they are, not as whom they want you to believe they are.

Many people don't want to bother with church today because they view the church as hypocritical. The people they see going to church say one thing, yet do something else.

They Say	They Do
Love thy neighbor.	Gossip about their neighbor, ignore their neighbor, put down their neighbor.
Jesus washes away our sins.	If you don't look or act a certain way, you don't belong. Acting or talking as if they are "holier" than others.
Jesus loves the little children.	Violate or ignore the young.
We are all God's children.	Divisive behavior and discrimination.
Jesus brings life.	Dead, lifeless worship and pessimistic outlooks.

It breaks my heart to see people who say they are Christians doing things that a disciple of Christ wouldn't do. Jesus didn't seek out the powerful and the popular. He didn't seek to create a new popular crowd but instead sought to create a new world order; one based on unconditional love.

People experience so much hypocrisy and posturing in the real world. The last place they want to experience it is in the house of God; the place of healing; the place that is supposed to be the church. And so we need authentic constructs, genuine relationships. We need to do away with preconceived notions and replace them with potent, life-giving interactions.

> Real church happens when hypocrisy gives way to wholeness, truth takes over falsehood

Someone who has just been released from their begging state has no time or patience for phony or fake conditions. There is one thing about people who are done living a lie or who are searching for something real: they can instantly tell if something is fake, phony or a derivative of what it should be.

Mind you now, all of us are hypocrites because there is usually a lag between when we decide on something and when we act on that knowledge. At some point in time in our lives, and if we are honest with ourselves, numerous times, we say one thing and do another or we do one thing and say another.

Healed beggars are searching for a place and, most importantly, for a people who have the courage to acknowledge their shortcomings, the boldness to confess their issues, the willingness to be open about their lives. They are searching for a people who are open about their struggles and successes, their failures and victories and who have the desire to help one another pursue a holistic life.

Real church happens when hypocrisy gives way to wholeness, truth takes over falsehood; when "just as I am without one plea…" is not just a hymn sung on Sunday, but is a daily practice in the life of the church.

Have you ever looked at someone and known they are pretending to be someone they are not? You can tell by the careful façade and glib conversations that they aren't dealing with whoever it is that they really are, or whatever it is that they really think. Hypocrites say one thing and do another. They judge others while they are guilty too (and sometimes of things far worse). Sometimes a hypocrite is just trying to cover up his or her own perceived inadequacies. They might get caught up in intellectual gibberish that gives the appearance of brilliance but severely lacks the content or the heart of intelligence. Ultimately these people will condemn those that do "x" while they, too, do "x". And all of that gets wrapped up in the fear of losing status.

The root of hypocrisy is the fear of being judged by others and falling short. That fear fills the vacuum created by the absence of a real relationship with Jesus Christ.

We need to find environments that invite people to come as they are with NO fear of condemnation or judgment. We all need real churches where we can bring our stuff and our messes and be blessed. As many real churches say: We want you to come as you are, but we love you too much to let you stay in areas and situations of brokenness. Real churches include people who have come to grips with their faults, and yet, have found in Jesus forgiveness, freedom and the fortitude to move forward. Real churches include those who understand that they see people for what they can be, not for what they are.

When Jesus becomes real to me, then I know that He has become acquainted with my faults and failures, my sufferings and shortcomings, my trials and my temptations. And I have become acquainted with His ability to heal, forgive and constantly help me to start over again.

Once we accept that we no longer have to be concerned with hiding our defects from the public eye, we then can concern ourselves with finding an environment and people who can help us be more than we ever thought we could be.

When I get to that point, then the fact that I used to be promiscuous can be overcome by the reality that I am a liberator. The fact that I used to be a liar and cheater is overcome by the reality that I'm a transformer in the name of Jesus. The fact that I still struggle with various deficiencies of character is overtaken by the fact that I am on a journey to wholeness and that I will be better tomorrow than I am today. And I am not what I was yesterday, by the grace of God.

So how do you achieve this authenticity? You have to have failed and watched Jesus lift you back up. You have to have fallen short and witnessed the Lord carry you the extra mile. You have to have gotten knocked down and then overcome public embarrassment, shame and guilt that resulted from your actions. You have to reach a point with Jesus where you are not concerned about what others think. Nor are you worried about what others might say. But instead your sole focus is on learning about Jesus, following Jesus and living a life that loves Him, loves others and loves yourself as well as possible. All pride, all pretence and all image-maintaining behavior has got to go out the window. You have to get to a point where you realize that the only thing that has gotten through is the grace and power of God.

My authenticity is being developed in many ways. But one profound way was through my grieving experience after losing my father to a sudden heart attack. When my dad died, my life collapsed. Physically, my body shut down in moments of stress and fatigue that no excuse or cover up could hide. Emotionally and mentally, I slipped into a mild depression that no rationalizing or reasoning could explain away. Finances fractured my family. Many of the unresolved issues that we as a family kept private because we were taught to keep private, day by day became more exposed for the entire world to see. For example, my parents were not just separated, they were moving toward divorce and this was becoming public knowledge, even after a private cover-up. My mother was not the beloved wife or my dad the beloved husband anymore. They were estranged from one another. My sister had issues with our father, our mother and herself, and began looking for love in the wrong places. And me, well, I was the self-designated peacemaker, who while striving to work out my issues with my mother and father, found myself seeking to be the superman that I was not. In trying to keep all the family pieces together I found that, like Humpty Dumpty, they couldn't be put back together again. I had to examine who I was, who I was pretending to be, who I needed to be and most importantly whom God had made me to be in a climate of brokenness, lies, cover-ups and pain. But for the grace of God and a loving, stable wife, I would have crumbled under the intense pressure.

Being able to come to Jesus just as I am, even and especially at times when I'm beat down and broken, I am able to experience that He gives rest and peace of mind. I find that the only way out of stuff like that is to talk about it, to share it and to let people who really listen know what I am going through and that I need their prayers. When I discovered family, friends and even some church members who accepted me for me and helped me get over it, then that is when I started finding real church.

At a real church I don't have to hide behind masks of pretense. I can just show up without preparation. I can come to a fellowship and not have to hide anything. In fact the fellowship expects me to share my mess. It will accept me for who I am, for what I'm going through, and will help me continue to grow, to leave my begging state and become whole.

> At a real church I don't have to hide behind masks of pretense.

So how does a church show that it takes authenticity seriously? It puts people in leadership who are honest about and are working through their mess. For example, a couple of years ago, one of our talented ministry leads was moving with her husband to New Orleans. She recommended Linda Edwards as her replacement because she was a committed member of the ministry who had demonstrated the passion and desire to lead. The problem was that Linda was struggling with alcoholism. We decided to move forward with Linda as the leader because she was openly acknowledging her struggle and recognizing that it was Jesus who was pulling her through. People have gravitated toward her since then because they recognize her authentic nature.

Linda is far from perfect. She is still battling, but she is on the road to wholeness and people are rallying around her in support. If we continue to expect leaders to be perfect, we will perpetuate the tendency toward hypocrisy in our churches. On the other hand, if we expect leaders in the church to be transparent and on the journey to wholeness, we will get far more than we ever imagined.

Once the beggar was healed in Chapter 3 of *Acts* and went into the temple, we learn that the worshippers were amazed and astonished. By Chapter 4, the former beggar was in jail. By the end of Chapter 4, he had been set free. Being authentic will often make you unpopular. It is not comfortable and is rarely met with immediate applause. Because when you are being real you expose the unrealness around you by not only exposing the hypocrisy of others, but also by forcing them to deal with God and with themselves. Believe it or not, many people—even those in the traditional church—do not actually trust in the saving and liberating power of Jesus Christ and what this power can do for their lives. And so in fear they would rather persecute those who are authentic rather than embrace the authenticity that Jesus demands.

> When people show up authentically, a church has to be prepared for the level of discomfort and challenge that it often produces.

When people show up authentically, a church has to be prepared for the level of discomfort and challenge that it often produces.

In 1996, we made a conscious decision to reach out to homeless and street people in our neighborhood. We had never had any homeless people in church before, but we were compelled by our surroundings to open our doors to our neighbors. So we began inviting and feeding them when they came—spiritually and physically. Several of them took us up on our offer and they came to church stinking of drunkenness and urine. On one occasion, one of the men stole an usher's pocketbook, and on two occasions stole the hubcaps off of my car. On numerous occasions, a transvestite would come to visit and harass me personally to the point that I had to have three men guard my safety. One time, this individual cursed me out while I was serving communion. To make matters even worse, the church was frequently robbed. Things got so tense that one woman in our church said that we needed to build a fence around the church and not allow any of the street or homeless people in. I said, "No way. We need to open our doors even more." So we broadened our traditional housing program. We increased the number of feeding and clothing opportunities. We consecrated two street pastors, John Davis and Horace Dei, to put the word out on the street that we wanted to help people get back on their feet. And we declared that whosoever will, let them come.

When we had the courage to open our doors completely, the robberies stopped, some of the odor went away and a spirit of love began to invade the fellowship. Today, some of these individuals are our greatest inspirers and our greatest leaders. Without them, Emory would not be what it is daily.

The church is the body of baptized believers in Jesus. It is a body with many members. These members are anyone who believes that Jesus Christ is Savior and Lord. As members of this body, we have past issues in our lives. We have present issues in our lives. We are working through issues in our lives, but as long as we believe that Jesus can mold and shape our lives for the better, then God will work out and straighten those things that aren't quite in line with His vision for us.

I thank God every day that I can love Him, worship Him and walk with Him as He is molding and shaping me, getting the kinks out of me that don't need to be in me and, indeed, preparing me to be all that I can be in love and service to others.

> I serve a God who knows that I am a work in progress, and who is present to get me where He wants me to be.

I don't know about you, but I thank Him that I can live freely because He is my Lord and my Savior, that I can go through the washing machine of the Holy Ghost and that whatever does not come out in the wash, will come out in the rinse because I serve a God who knows that I am a work in progress, and who is present to get me where He wants me to be.

I want to be a member of that real church; not a phony church, not a pretentious church, not a church that puts on airs. I do not want

to be a part of a derivative church—a church that dresses up its stuff
to cover up its mess, but denies that it has had a mess all along. I want
to be a part of the real church—a church that is not caught up in posh
or pretense, but one that is sold out to help lives be saved physically,
emotionally, spiritually, relationally and financially. That's the church I
want to be a part of.

Ultimately, a church like this transforms. Because authentic folks
know that we will be vindicated. Though we may not be popular all the
time, we will be redeemed when trials come. Give me membership in
this kind of church, a real church.

God is trying to include anybody and everybody: whosoever
will, so let them come. So in real church, there are alcoholics who are
trying to straighten up and drug addicts who are trying to get sober.
There are those who do immoral things, who are trying to do the right
things. There are people with HIV/AIDS, who are still embraced by
the fellowship. There are adulterers, who are trying to have their slates
wiped clean. There are hypocrites, who are seeking an authentic life.
In real church there are ex-inmates, who have now become inmates
with Jesus.

In real church, everybody has a criminal record, even though some
have not been caught. In real church nobody is keeping tabs on our
wrongs because we know that all of us have wrongs, and that if God
added up all of our wrongs, there wouldn't be an ocean large enough
to contain them. But, in real church, we're just trying to be authentic,
transparent and real. With real church we know that our marriages
aren't quite where they ought to be, but if we hang in with God and
everybody, they will be what we need them to be. In real church we
understand that our dating record isn't quite what it ought to be, but
God can, in fact, straighten it up. In real church we understand that if
our salvation was dependent on what our checkbooks looked like, all of
us might go to hell.

But, in real church we understand that God is able to fix it, line it up
and do what needs to be done with it, in order for God to be glorified.
Is there anybody who wants to be part of real church? I want to be part
of a real church. In real church members aren't arguing over what type of
music should be sung because all of the music that God has created can

be sung to glorify His holy name. In real church the congregation is not hooked up or caught up in time constraints because they know that God is the author and the controller of time, and whenever God wants to start, we'll be there. And whatever God wants to end, we'll be there. And with everything in between, we'll give glory to God with it and in it. In a real church lives are changed. In a real church I can be my authentic self— who I really am. In a real church lives are transformed. In a real church when I'm at the bottom of the barrel, somebody is there to pick me back up again. In a real church somebody cares for me, somebody loves me, somebody is sold out for me.

A real church has the look of real love.

Time to Be REAL
(Relevant, Enthusiastic, Authentic and Loving)

1 In what ways are you hypocritical?

- What are you pretending to be that you are not?
- What are you hiding in order to preserve your status?
- Who do you judge and put down? What is it about them that might expose your own deficiencies or secrets?

2 What is one thing you can do right now to become more authentic?

3 If you are currently a member or part of a congregation, what one thing can you do to raise the level of authenticity?

4 If you are not currently attending a community of faith, start your search for an authentic one now. If you have made it this far in the book, we suspect that you have.

- At www.beggingforrealchurch.com download the "Real Church Checklist for Beggars" or visit a "real church" in your area. We have posted links to churches that others have told us are "real."
- If you find an authentic place that loves and forgives and accepts you for who you are and loves you too much to let you stay stuck in the habits, hurts and hang-ups that keep you from experiencing the love of God, please let us know!

Chapter 10:
Real Church
Loves

Show me a real church and I'll show you a church that loves with no strings attached. Show me a real church and I'll show you people who seek to be a visible example of God's love to the world.

There is confusion around the definition of love in our world; there is very little direct experience of unconditional love. When we say "God is love," we aren't talking about a Valentine's Day-Hallmark™-card-notes-passed-in-5th-grade kind of love. But we are talking about a kind of love that, at its core, is so concerned with the well-being of others that transformation and miracles are possible. A kind of love that is the anecdote to hypocrisy, complacency and superiority. Jesus calls this love *agape*.

There are many definitions of love in the world. But the one definition that ties all the other definitions together and makes some of them make sense is unconditional love—*agape*. Yet this definition is often ignored. I believe that this is the central reason why all of us, from time to time, struggle with love issues.

Churches often get hooked up in societal definitions of love, and we ignore the very source of love that our faith is grounded in which is *agape* love. *Agape* love is the passionate desire for the well-being of others. Not because they are worthy, but because God loves them, and God commands us to love them because God loves us when we are unworthy—God's love is not conditional on worthiness, or on anything else.

If we really understand what *agape* means, the other definitions of love would be handled with decency and in order. And our world, communities and churches crying out for help would find the very people of God helping them instead of hurting them, practicing justice instead of injustice, conquering marginalization instead of perpetuating it. Without *agape* love, the other kinds of love can—and often do—run wild. Leading to disorder, disruption and chaos in our families, communities and relationships—our world.

> Without agape love, the other kinds of love can—and often do—run wild.

Eros (sexual) love without *agape* leads to a selfish, sexual passion that often is damaging and abusive in relationships. Maniac love without *agape* love is a roller coaster ride that can lead to crimes of passion or terrorism. Philanthropic love without *agape* love might give, but to the wrong causes or for the wrong reasons—with strings attached. And lack of love leads to wars, rumors of war and constant fear.

Agape, God's love, has to be the focus. Because when we focus on the well-being of other people, God has a way of making sure that our well-being is taken care of. So a real church is passionate about living out this love in the communities in which they find themselves. A real church recognizes that Jesus loves us like this. And without this kind of love running rampant, peace, harmony and justice for all is impossible.

Paul wrote a letter to the people of Corinth to remind and to teach them the kind of love that God extends and expects us to extend. The reason he wrote this letter is that word got back to him that the people of Corinth were fighting over superficial things (e.g., which spiritual gift was better, who was greater, etc.) instead of keeping the main thing the main thing. Here is Peterson's translation of this letter:

> [1] *If I speak with human eloquence and angelic ecstasy but don't love, I'm nothing but the creaking of a rusty gate.* [2] *If I*

speak God's Word with power, revealing all His mysteries and making everything plain as day, and if I have faith that says to a mountain, "Jump," and it jumps, but I don't love, I'm nothing. ³⁻⁷ If I give everything I own to the poor and even go to the stake to be burned as a martyr, but I don't love, I've gotten nowhere. So, no matter what I say, what I believe, and what I do, I'm bankrupt without love.

Love never gives up.
Love cares more for others than for self.
Love doesn't want what it doesn't have.
Love doesn't strut,
Doesn't have a swelled head,
Doesn't force itself on others,
Isn't always "me first,"
Doesn't fly off the handle,
Doesn't keep score of the sins of others,
Doesn't revel when others grovel,
Takes pleasure in the flowering of truth,
Puts up with anything,
Trusts God always,
Always looks for the best,
Never looks back,
But keeps going to the end.

⁸⁻¹⁰Love never dies. Inspired speech will be over some day; praying in tongues will end; understanding will reach its limit. We know only a portion of the truth, and what we say about God is always incomplete. But when the Complete arrives, our incompletes will be canceled. ¹³But for right now, until that completeness, we have three things to do to lead us toward that consummation: Trust steadily in God, hope unswervingly, love extravagantly. And the best of the three is love.
From 1 Corinthians 13

If the main thing is going to be the main thing, real churches must love and must teach people how to love. Paul taught the unruly people of Corinth (and us) how to love through this letter of encouragements and unity. He talked about these in four simple ways:

Abide in God and allow God to reside in you. You can't really love somebody unless the love of God abides in you. You can't really love somebody unless the love of God is bubbling up in you and is sweating out of your pores. John in his letters supports Paul's letter by saying that to love, God must abide in us. He used the example of Jesus being the vine and we being the branches. How long do you think the leaves on a branch stay alive once the branch is cut away from the vine?

> Real churches must love and must teach people how to love.

Extend patience and kindness. When you exercise, there are two primary ways to work the muscles: contract or extend. Contraction means that the muscles are pulled in. God does not want us to pull in or be selfish or self-contained. God wants us to extend, to open and to share ourselves with others. This requires great discipline and apparatuses because the extended position requires more control. In like manner, it takes control to begin to express love even when evil is coming for us. Kindness is the ability to abstain or control ourselves when wronged, while expressing love to the offender in the process. Patience is the ability to bear pain or trials calmly and without complaint.

Prune the eight things that block love. To prune is to cut back so that something can grow. The only way to love is to let go of stuff or allow God to prune away the things that block the flow of love. If I'm going to love, I must constantly remove eight attitudes that attack love. God does not abide in us powerfully if these eight attitudes are present. If God abides in you, this stuff can't live in you because love and loveless behavior can't exist in the same place. One or the other has to be evicted.

The eight attitudes that sought to tear up the Corinthian church and community seem to be timeless because they still affect us today:

1. Jealousy – hostility shown toward a rival, or toward one who has an advantage, or toward one who is more gifted in a particular area than you are, or toward one who has been unfaithful.
2. Boasting – to speak of or assert with excessive pride, to brag or to flaunt at the expense of others. To brag about what you have at the expense of others who don't have.
3. Arrogance – puffed up, exaggerating one's own worth or importance in an overbearing manner.
4. Rudeness – offensive in manner or action; unfinished, uncouth, unrefined, uncivilized, unlearned, discourteous.
5. Self-centeredness – concerned only with one's own desires.
6. Irritability – to annoy, to show impatience, anger or displeasure in.
7. Resentful – to feel or express annoyance or ill will, to keep a record or account of the slights experienced and then plan payback.
8. Rejoicing in wrong – pleasure or desire in gossip that tears somebody down or in failures.

Adopt five eternal attitudes. As learners and followers of Jesus, we've been postured to bring good news into people's lives, not bad news. And so, therefore, to love we've got to be able to:

- Rejoice in the truth (takes pleasure in righteousness) – to celebrate and encourage doing the right thing.
- Bear all things (puts up with anything) – to move while holding up or supporting; to put up with, sustain, tolerate.
- Believe all things (trusts God always) – to hold dear, to love, to like, to desire, to see the possibilities in someone or something, even when things look impossible.
- Hope all things (always looks for the best) – to wish, to expect, to look forward to, to leap in expectation, to hope for the best even when hope can't be seen.
- Endure all things (never looks back, but keeps going to the end) – remains firm under suffering or misfortune without yield, continues to undergo hardship without giving in.

My Aunt Elsie and my Aunt Betty have become each other's support network in the face of tremendous adversity and love. My Aunt Elsie's and Uncle Cornish's lives turned upside down when their son, David, a pediatric geneticist, had a horrific accident. David was driving on the freeway on his way to take his dad to a birthday dinner when a wheel from a car travelling on the other side of the freeway came off and bounced over the median to the side where my cousin was driving. The wheel came through the roof of the car and literally crushed him. To make a long story short, my cousin became a quadriplegic. For the last 23 years he has been dependent upon my aunt and uncle and a team of loyal aides. After a long and remarkable recovery, David has been able to live a quality life and resume doing everything he was positioned to do professionally: he is a nationally-recognized geneticist, sees patients, does research, writes papers and teaches. His doctors didn't think he'd make it past the age of 50, but he is now 53 and going strong—thanks be to God. Obviously, Aunt Elsie, Uncle Cornish and David had to have a tremendous amount of love: bearing, believing, hoping and enduring lots of things. My aunt and uncle have lovingly sacrificed their plans and dreams for their son.

My Aunt Betty's story parallels that of my Aunt Elsie. As sisters who have been close all of their lives, their respective tragedies have caused them to have a bond that cannot be broken. My Aunt Betty is the picture of endurance. She continues to rejoice, bear, believe, hope and endure in spite of:

- A daughter being born mentally retarded.
- Being the primary caregiver for my grandmother, her mother, for 15 years, through brain operations and strokes, until she died.
- My dad dying at 56, my dad being Betty's best friend outside of her husband.
- Her husband, Earl, suddenly dying of stomach cancer two years later at the young age of 60.
- Being the primary caregiver for my grandfather, who died of cancer at the age of 89.
- Two of her kids lost their way and are struggling to try and find

it. One to drug addiction and alcoholism, the other is locked behind bars.

- Learning that she had breast cancer, undergoing a mastectomy and—thanks be to God—is now living as a survivor.

After years of struggle and loss, she's still loving and on fire for the Lord.

Paul makes it very clear that there are no shortcuts in loving the way God wants us to love. Loving like this, *agape*, is a process. It doesn't come overnight, but people and churches that embark upon the journey are those that find themselves transforming lives daily. Real churches begin the journey and real churches live out the journey because real churches love. When we love like this, we will find ourselves committed to God and to others.

For just as human love oftentimes leads to marriage, God's love leads to commitment. What would you say if God asked you: *Will you marry me?* In the context of a real church, when you make the commitment to marry God, you are making the commitment to unconditionally love others. And others who have married God have made a commitment to unconditionally love you. Because if you marry God, I marry you. And if you marry God, you marry me. This type of commitment says you desire my well-being above all else. And I marry you with a commitment that says I desire your well-being above all else because I'm married to God.

> What would you say if God asked you: Will you *marry* me?

In real church, people are tired of dating God, but instead want to marry God. They are not looking to plan a fairytale wedding, but rather an authentic, transparent one. Imagine asking someone in a real church:

- Will you marry me with my stuff?
- Will you marry me with my issues?
- Will you marry me with all of the good things I can show the world and offer you?
- Will you marry me with the junk that gets on your last nerve? With your only nerve? The nerve that hurts the most when somebody steps on it?
- Neighbor, will you marry me?

The metaphor of marriage may not sit well with everyone. There are many people who have experienced the painful wounds of divorce and separation. However, just because you may be divorced from a partner doesn't mean that you need to be divorced from God. Nor does it mean that you need to divorce yourself from the principles that form a healthy, happy, life-changing marriage with God.

Just like people have felt frustrated in the institution of marriage, people have felt frustrated in the institution of the church. Just because you have experienced betrayal, hurt and/or disappointment in the setting of a particular church doesn't mean that you need to divorce God. In fact, like in any healthy marriage there are good moments and bad moments, good times and bad times. There are seasons of pure bliss where your spouse can do no wrong and seasons of pure misery where your spouse can do no right. The great R & B group, Frankie Beverly and Maze, would call it *"Joy and pain are like sunshine and rain."*

Such it is in a marriage with God. There are seasons when it is hot and seasons when it is cold. And even seasons where it is lukewarm, but the God we married is unchanging, ever faithful, ever compassionate and eternally patient. God understands that we go through these seasons. In a real church, when the relationship is hot, Got wants it hotter. When it is cold, God seeks to rekindle the fire. God is always seeking to draw us closer for a deeper, more intimate, increasingly authentic relationship with the very core of God's being—unconditional love.

> *God never gives up.*
> *God cares more for others than for self.*
> *God doesn't want what God doesn't have.*
> *God doesn't strut,*
> *God doesn't have a swelled head,*
> *Doesn't force itself on others,*
> *Isn't always "me first,"*
> *Doesn't fly off the handle,*
> *Doesn't keep score of the sins of others,*
> *Doesn't revel when others grovel,*
> *Takes pleasure in the flowering of truth,*

Puts up with anything,
Always looks for the best,
Never looks back,
But keeps going to the end.

At The Emory Fellowship, our mission is to be a visible example of God's love, leading people to Christ-centered wholeness. Like many mission statements, it reflects our commitment, hopes and intentions. It doesn't mean that we fulfill our mission in every interaction, but we are working and praying our way toward it. We are not a perfect church (no church is), but we are a church that seeks to use our mission statement as a litmus test for whether or not we are being real.

One idea that we had was to employ some of the homeless men in our area to clean up the streets. For us, this gave them a job. It also was a "visible example" that could not only lead those working to a Christ-centered wholeness through Bible study, counseling and prayer, as well as work, but has also become a way to reach other homeless folks and bring them wholeness just the same. Many of them have joined the fellowship.

In fact, many guests comment on the feeling of welcome and warmth they experience at our worship services. We view the time of greeting one another in the love and grace of God as an opportunity to be a visible example of love. When describing her first visit to Emory to her friends, one of our young people said: "I just hugged and was hugged by 12 people I didn't used to know." Another guest said, "After the seventh hug, you had me. I was left in tears of joy."

To God, there are no strangers. There is no North or South. There is no East and no West. There is no young and no old. There is no black and no white. God's love is for ALL.

Time to Be REAL
(Relevant, Enthusiastic, Authentic and Loving)

1 You are a child of God. As such, you have unconditional love in you. Read through Paul's definition of love one more time. But this time, insert your name every place he used the word "love."

- *(Your Name)* never gives up.
- *(Your Name)* cares more for others than for self.
- *(Your Name)* doesn't want what it doesn't have.
- *(Your Name)* doesn't strut, doesn't have a swelled head,
- *(Your Name)* doesn't force itself on others,
- *(Your Name)* isn't always "me first,"
- *(Your Name)* doesn't fly off the handle,
- *(Your Name)* doesn't keep score of the sins of others,
- *(Your Name)* doesn't revel when others grovel,
- *(Your Name)* takes pleasure in the flowering of truth,
- *(Your Name)* puts up with anything,
- *(Your Name)* trusts God always,
- *(Your Name)* always looks for the best,
- *(Your Name)* never looks back, but keeps going to the end.

2 As you read the above, there were probably aspects that rang more true for you than others. Which aspects of love do you need to better learn from your heavenly father and mother (*i.e.*, God)? Say a simple prayer right now asking for guidance and strength.

3 If you are not a part of a real church, find one that will love you: www.beggingforrealchurch.com

Chapter 11
Real Church Forgives

Show me a real church and I'll show you a church that doesn't hold your past or present against you. Show me a real church and I'll show you a people who remind you that forgiveness is around the corner.

In Chapter 10, we talked a bit about real love. One of the major barriers to experiencing and sharing unconditional love is the fact that we don't forgive others, and we often don't forgive ourselves. The principle of forgiveness is core to the life and ministry of Jesus.

> Peter replied, "Repent and be baptized, every one of you, in the name of Jesus Christ for the forgiveness of your sins. And you will receive the gift of the Holy Spirit. The promise is for you and your children and for all who are far off—for all whom the Lord our God will call."[13]

In this scripture, our receipt of God's power is contingent on two basic steps. The first is repentance, which means turning away from sin, evil or wrongdoing and turning our lives God-ward. It's like making a 180-degree turn away from the things that cause evil, division, dissension and despair, and turning toward the things that cause peace, harmony, love, joy and happiness. The second step is Baptism. This is a symbol or statement to the world that you have turned God-ward and have decided to follow Jesus Christ. Our sins are washed away in body and spirit.

Peter says that when these two moves of one's mind, heart and actions take place, then forgiveness is rendered completely and God's power is unleashed. Remember God's forgiveness is complete, not partial. No traces remain. God washes away what happened from His record and tells us to move forward unburdened. It's like walking on a beach and having your footprints in the sand washed away by the crashing waves on the shore. There is no remnant of what happened. Likewise no remnant of wrongdoing remains when God forgives us.

Many people struggle with the fact that God loves us like that. Many people have trouble wrapping their arms around this Grace-filled concept. But the reality is that this is how God loves and this is how God encourages us to love.

I'd be the first to tell you that it is very difficult to forgive people who have done you wrong. Forgiveness truly is a process and usually doesn't happen overnight. When bad things have happened to us or bad things have been done to us, it takes determination and effort to forgive. When we have caused or inflicted harm on others, it also takes work to get to the place of forgiveness personally. Sometimes we blame God. Sometimes we blame others. Sometimes we blame ourselves. We ask questions like: "Why do bad things happen to good people?" or "Why would God let me get sick?" or worse, "Why would God allow anything evil to happen to a child?" The list goes on and on. But as we release our guilt, pain, shame, bitterness and resentment for others and ourselves, God is able to replenish our souls with the hope and expectation of great things to come.

I remember holding a tremendous sense of bitterness and anger toward one of my colleagues. We had agreed to enter a business endeavor together while we were in divinity school. There were certain guarantees and certain timelines that we had committed to one another. When it came time for us to fulfill our obligation to one another, my colleague decided to back out. Thousands of dollars were involved, as well as family plans and goals. Even more painful, a friendship was severely compromised. For a long time I felt like beating him up or planning some sort of retaliation that would do him harm. I carried this bitterness with me for almost two years. It began to sour my witness, particularly in settings with people who knew the two of us.

When forgiveness is demanded of us and we refuse to offer it, we become bitter and our health, our mindset and our relationships with others are sorely affected. I found that this very thing was causing me to suffer. I wasn't able to release it until a dear friend of mine intervened. He called me one night and challenged me, then prayed for me to let it go, to release it. That night I did, and immediately I felt the weight of the world taken off of my shoulders.

Because I forgave my colleague, I have been able to treat him with love in spite of what he did to me because I let God handle the barriers that developed between us. Because I forgave my colleague, my physical, emotional and spiritual health was strengthened and I discovered God restoring to me everything I lost and much more. Today, while our relationship is not the same as before, there is peace between us. Nothing beats being able to live with peace of mind, body and soul.

> No remnant of wrongdoing remains when God forgives us.

Many beggars who believe in God struggle with a lack of forgiving. And like the beggar in *Acts 3,* it leads us to being stuck, lame and unable to move. God wants to unleash His unbelievable, amazing power and possibilities upon each of us. He is ready to do it right now. But we must choose to forgive.

God wants to restore a broken family, tarnished marriage or friendship. God wants to start a new career in you, or return you to a healthy and vibrant lifestyle. But until you choose to repent, be forgiven and forgive others, God will not do what God wants to do in your life. And that is not on God. That is on us.

Especially in the fellowship of believers, as my story above reveals, forgiveness is required. Many churches are compromised in their ability to transform lives and communities because they have chosen to hold onto grudges, divisions and bad memories. They wage internal fights and battles between each other because people in the fellowship have not forgiven or received forgiveness from others. Think of all the wasted opportunities churches have to define the great things that can happen in the lives of children, women and men in cities, communities and countries because we won't forgive. When we choose to forgive, wars will be brought to an end, some wars will never be started, poverty will be reduced, hardships relieved, economies revitalized, violence removed and opportunity instead of waste will fill our streets.

> Without forgiving and feeling that we are forgiven, we paint ourselves in a corner far away from God and others who love us unconditionally.

Real churches make the right choices. Real churches choose to forgive. In Hebrew culture, out of which much of the Bible was based, the word forgiveness literally means to release—to let go, to give up something or somebody that is not healthy for you. Real churches are filled with people who are constantly letting go, and are moving to make amends with people they have hurt.

Many people ignore the fact that the ability to forgive has so many spiritual and physical health ramifications. Doctors and nurses will tell you that 80% of all physical ailments are spiritually and mentally related. I would contend that the reason for much of this is because there are issues, problems and challenges too great for us to handle by ourselves that we have needed to release to God by faith, but instead we have chosen to hold onto them. As a result, our minds and bodies cannot handle the tremendous stress this causes, and we break down unnecessarily. When we forgive, we feel better and we are better.

Have you ever been in a situation where you couldn't identify enough choices to be able to find a good way out of a problem? Having choice and being at a place of choice is a luxury that those who are oppressed, downtrodden, depressed or addicted simply do not have. Without forgiveness, our freedom of choice is reduced. If we don't forgive our mom for something she said that made us feel unworthy as a child, we don't have the choice to have a good relationship with her. If we don't forgive ourselves for striking out in anger, we don't have a choice to see ourselves as capable of peace.

Without forgiving and feeling that we are forgiven, we paint ourselves in a corner far away from God and others who love us unconditionally. If we think that "God allowed" us to get cancer, we might not feel we have the choice to pray to that same God for strength and for healing. If we think God is punishing us by taking the life of someone we love, we don't have the choice to fully understand and experience the nature of God. If we think that the church is a safe haven for pedophiles and that somehow God condones that, we might not have the choice to trust God or the church.

Some people don't forgive themselves as completely as God forgives them. Others don't buy into the concept of forgiveness because they think that it is always tied to the notion of forgetfulness. "Forgive and forget" might work for a minor infraction or altercation (*e.g.*, someone pushed you down accidentally) but doesn't apply to major ones (e.g., domestic abuse). But understand, God doesn't ask us to forget. He created us with minds and memories, and forgetting is often hard to do. What God asks us to do is forgive. And as we forgive, we will find God handling the memories and moving us to wholeness in spite of them.

One of the visible ways a real church communicates this full-blown, love-based reality of forgiveness is through telling their stories of trials and salvation. The beggar jumped up praising God and he goes to church.

When we forgive and are forgiven, we are able to see visions and dream dreams that are larger than ourselves, and we are able to accomplish those greater things through the grace and direction of Jesus Christ.

Time to Be REAL
(Relevant, Enthusiastic, Authentic and Loving)

❶ Make a list of your top three grudges. Those things that have happened to you that hurt you physically, emotionally, socially or spiritually.

❷ Pick one. Find a friend who seems to be exceptionally good at letting go and letting God. Ask him or her to help you find your way with God through letting go of your identified grudges.

❸ Now make a list of your top three regrets about things you did not try because you couldn't identify enough choices to make a clear decision. What have you learned from these regrets?

❹ Pick one. Find a friend who seems to be exceptionally good at saying they are sorry and letting God heal the guilt.

Chapter 12
Real Church Breaks Barriers & Builds Bridges

S how me a real church and I'll show you a church that actively tears down barriers. Show me a real church and I'll show you a people who serve as bridges between the Giver of Life and the living dead.

I have a daughter who attends college in Long Island, NY. When I pick her up with my SUV and bring all of her belongings back home for the summer, the number of bridges I have to cross intrigues me. Mind you now, most of my time seems to be spent in New York. I can get from Silver Spring, MD to Staten Island in three hours. Somebody once said, "You're flying." I told them, "No, I'm driving." I can get there in three hours, and on one occasion, I literally got to the Belt Parkway right across the Verrazano Bridge in three hours. But occassionally, I hit New York at the wrong time. I got there once at 3:00 p.m. and then it took me three hours to go 70 miles to Joia's campus. It took me *three* hours just to get from the Verrazano Bridge to Suffolk County.

But I'm fascinated because there are three bridges that I have to cross, and I don't like bridges because I'm scared of heights. And so whenever I cross a bridge, I'm trying to cross in the middle lane so that I don't have to look too far to my right or my left.

The first bridge I cross on my journey to New York is the Delaware Memorial Bridge, which intimidates me every time I see it. I then choose to cross, not the Goethals Bridge, but the Outerbridge Crossing, which gets me into New York a little sooner. That bridge connects New Jersey to Staten Island, New York. But the big mama is the Verrazano. Every time I go across the Verrazano I pray because that is a huge, intimidating bridge.

But what fascinates me about bridges is that without them, there are people and regions that would always be disconnected from one another. Unless you had a boat to get from one place to another, you'd never be able to talk, share, interact, rejoice, join in fellowship with, or somehow discover that God has a far bigger world out there than just your own place and mine.

Who do you need to build a bridge with today?

In the book of *Acts* we see God's kind of bridge building. Among many things, the Lord used the opportunity at Pentecost to break barriers of language, ethnicity, culture and religion—to mention a few—in order to bring people together in a common union with Jesus Christ and one another through the power of the Holy Spirit. Like a bridge, God connected people who otherwise would have had little or no interaction.

And what God desires us to do as real church then is to connect with people who do not speak our language or look like us or act like us or talk like us, but who still have the presence of God in them just the same. Because if we connect with them, God has a broader, more fascinating, more powerful experience for our lives.

God can reach more people worldwide and locally, and bring hope, healing, deliverance and liberation to them if we will simply build the bridge. Who do you need to build a bridge with today? Because real church is about building bridges, it's not about building or keeping barriers in place.

In real church, bridges are built and barriers are broken because God gives us a common language that unifies people instead of dividing us in the midst of our differences. That common language is the language of unconditional love.

If I'm building bridges, God gives me the ability to talk to anybody in love and the ability to talk in their language. For example, I can talk to the gang bangers and the hiphop culture when I'm given the ability to speak their language. I can talk to the gay-lesbian community when the Lord gives me the ability to speak in their language. I can speak to any immigrant culture in their language when God gives me the ability. I may not be able to be a master in Spanish or French or Shona or Swahili, but I can find, through the help of God, a common language that allows us to come together as people.

We humans seem to specialize in building up barriers to keep us separated instead of building bridges. We'll spend more energy on trying to keep those barriers up than we will on trying to tear them down. We can feel it right in our own backyard.

We are currently fighting two wars with people who don't look like most of us, speak our language or practice religion that is familiar to most of us. We are in an immigration battle in this nation, which threatens to tear us apart at the core because we insist on having different rules for different people. We fight every year around the anniversary of *Roe v. Wade* because one side is "pro-life" the other is "pro-choice," and rarely do we search for the common ground. Even after electing the first black president in our nation's history, racism is still rampant across America.

We still fight in our churches, even "kill" people during morning worship services. We battle over which denomination is the right denomination. We still haven't found a peaceful resolution to the gay-lesbian controversy that is real in our churches, our politics and every one of our communities.

Speaking of politics, we have Democratic barriers and Republican barriers. In fact, we have barriers within parties. There are conservative and liberal divisions.

There are barriers even in the institutional church. We can't even come together as a church. We have United Methodists, Baptists, Lutherans, Catholics, Episcopalians and Presbyterians, etc. And we divide ourselves over silly stuff. Some cry out, "You did not baptize me by immersing me!" As if immersing is the only way of baptism. Many believe that sprinkling is the only way. And we divide. I'm not averse to sprinkling, immersing or pouring. Why? Because I have a broader theological understanding. I understand that the water is symbolic of cleansing, but unless you have been bathed, soaked or saturated in the power of the Holy Ghost, you can go down a wet devil and come up a wet devil. You can be sprinkled like a wet devil, poured on like a wet devil and still be a wet devil when you leap up out of the water. You have to have God. You have to have God's love alive in you.

Bridges need to be built and barriers need to be broken down because we've got too much division in this world. We have people arguing over stupid stuff when we need to be looking at broader stuff. We have people dividing and separating over foolishness. Yet if we would just talk to one another, we'd be all right.

Real churches build bridges and break down barriers. Real churches do this inside and outside the four walls. Real churches practice bridge-building love on Capitol Hill, in the hallways of government, in communities, in places and in spaces where people think the church is not supposed to be. Real churches stand up with the authority of God and declare what the Lord says—that God is a God of peace, not war; that God is a God who turns our swords into plowshares; that God is the Able One who can bring all things back together again.

That's the practical language of real church. What language needs to inform your actions today? What tongue needs to be on your lips? Do you need to go to your spouse and say, "I'm sorry for the mess up, but I'm building a bridge of peace to you right now in the name of Jesus so that there would be peace in our relationship and peace in our home?" Is it that bridge?

Is it a bridge that needs to go to a brother or a sister who you haven't spoken to in years, but is crying out for love, mercy and affection, and you are the one who is to give it to them? You simply need to build a bridge over to them, to let them know that yes, there is a bridge over troubled waters and His name is Jesus the Christ. What bridge do you need to build today?

Do we need to build a bridge into a community we haven't touched yet—a community crying out for our help and our service? Do we need to reach back and build a bridge with those who we left back home in our native land, but who are suffering and who need a saving word or the presence of God to come into the fellowship in a great and mighty way?

A real church is not a real church unless it is relevant in its community. A place where people are coming out from behind the four walls and engaging in the lives of the people who live, work and exist in the community. An authentic encounter moves into a meaningful engagement that produces radical expectations from within the very people who once were hopeless, but now see possibility with the church in community. At Emory this has meant helping homeless people find jobs and housing. This has meant helping immigrants achieve citizenship or legal status. This has meant helping small businesses not just survive, but thrive. This has meant supporting at-risk youth through afterschool programming, entrepreneurship and periodic events that allow these young people to see that the world is bigger and brighter than their own neighborhood. These are just some of the ways that Emory has sought to be real in its own community. I can honestly say now what I could not say ten years ago: if our congregation left the Brightwood community today, we would be sorely missed in our neighborhood and city. We would be missed for our worship, our services, our efforts to radically extend our hearts and hands to help people become whole and we would be missed for the bridges we continue to build between the hopeless and the hope-filled.

> A real church is not a real church unless it is relevant in its community.

What bridge do you need to build today? What language do you need to speak? Do you need to learn how to speak a hip-hop culture language? Do you need to be able to rap like Kanye West, or at least understand what Kanye West is trying to tell a hip-hop culture today so that you might put a Holy Ghost spin on that which he misses?

In the book of *Acts*, 3,000 people came running to the life Jesus offered because suddenly real church was taking place. Real church was building bridges and it was knocking down barriers.

The power of the real church in *Acts 2* is that they were constantly giving and sacrificing themselves for others. This is the essence of self-giving and *agape* love, and is the essential ingredient in bridge building. Because this love was being practiced, *Acts 2* informs us that daily there were people who were becoming a part of the real church. The reason this was happening was that everyday people were seeing that someone in the world cared for them as much as they cared for themselves. I want to be a part of a church that thinks and acts like this. That cares for others as much as it cares for itself.

Real church breaks barriers of selfishness and self-centeredness. One of the greatest challenges for churches today is that too many are turning inward. Who is going to bother coming to be a part of a church where everything they talk about and do has nothing to do with the individual who comes in the door for the first time, or with the beggars who are sitting outside the church door? What beggars need and what beggars are looking for is a congregation whose mind is on the people in the street—literally and figuratively. People in the street are hungering and thirsting for something beyond themselves because in finding something beyond themselves, they will find meaning to their own lives. And so a real church that preaches love, teaches love, and then practices love—desiring the well-being of others—becomes a magnet for those searching for greater meaning.

> Real church breaks barriers of selfishness and self-centeredness.

When we begin to build a bridge, we engage people to start looking at others. When you look at the needs of others, suddenly you become engaged with something larger than yourself, and God begins to take you into spaces and places that are larger than you can even imagine. This gives people a sense of meaning. You are invited to love and be loved. Only in allowing unconditional love to have its way can barriers be broken and lasting bridges be built.

Real church builds bridges and breaks down barriers.

Time to Be REAL
(Relevant, Enthusiastic, Authentic and Loving)

1 What bridges do you most need to begin building today?

2 What are three simple things you can do to get started?

3 What barriers are getting in the way of living a real, authentic life-giving existence?

Conclusion:
So What's Your Story?

Show me a real church and I'll show you a church that has a passion for begging. Show me a real church and I'll show you a people whose begging leads to continual blessing not prolonged brokenness.

We began this journey together hoping that this book would serve as a catalyst for leading broken beggars to a new life of blessing. Our hope, our prayer and our desire was that people from all walks of life, who are experiencing brokenness of any sort, would find wholeness in Jesus Christ our Lord. That people would be:

- Well physically,
- Healed emotionally,
- Opened and Obedient to the movement of God's Spirit,
- Loved unconditionally and
- Empowered financially.

We know by our own lives that transformation is a process. But hopefully, after reading this book, you see that transformation in the name of Jesus is very much possible for you.

To a large degree we never stop begging and, truth be told, we should never stop begging. For God has more blessings to bestow upon us so that we can be a greater blessing to others. If we stop begging in this capacity, we miss out on so many blessings that God eagerly desires to unleash upon us and upon others. The key is whom you beg to, what you beg for and how you beg for it. If you are begging for Jesus to work out His full and perfect will for your life, then all that you beg for will come to pass. Jesus promised this in John's Gospel[14], "If you remain in me and my words remain in you, ask whatever you wish, and it will be given you." The question for you is, does your begging perpetuate your brokenness

> To a large degree we never stop begging and, truth be told, we should never stop begging.

or does your begging create blessing for you and others? My hope is that the latter defines your begging.

That can happen by having an authentic encounter with God, an ongoing meaningful engagement with our Lord, and living with the radical expectation that at any moment Jesus is able to do with your life what He said He would do.

A friend of mine named Suzette used to beg in a manner that perpetuated her brokenness. Frustrated with her high–paying career, her dysfunctional family and low self-esteem, Suzette made it a habit of drinking her way to numbness. Suzette is not your typical street drunk. She lives in a great neighborhood, drives a sweet car and projects an image of success. She is the hidden beggar that so many of us never see and that so many of us are. We want hope but are trapped in despair and dead ends.

> The question for you is, does your begging perpetuate your brokenness or does your begging create blessing for you and others?

Suzette, however, decided to make a life change. Angry with the direction her life was going, she started going to AA meetings, found a pastor she could trust, a preacher who taught about Jesus' message of deliverance on a regular basis and discovered a congregation that loved her unconditionally. Through it all she had an authentic encounter with Jesus.

Not that she didn't know about Jesus before...after all, she grew up in a family that believed in God. But now, because of this authentic encounter that led to meaningful engagement, she knows Jesus for herself and lives every day with the radical expectation that life is going to get better and better. And it is. Just the other day, Suzette celebrated two years of sobriety. She is now begging for God's greater blessing: blessings of joy, peace of mind, and an ordered and abundant life. Once the picture of misery, she is now a portrait of God's grace and mercy.

Like Suzette, Jimmy has traded broken begging for blessed begging. Jimmy once had a very prosperous and successful life working in business, but a series of bad decisions, extended lines of credit and reckless living led to a crisis of major proportions. Things got so bad for Jimmy that for a period of time he lived at friends' houses, in cars and in situations that would remind you of Will Smith in the movie *The Pursuit of Happyness*. And yet, after a chance encounter with a complete stranger on a bus, he learned about a church that could respond to his greatest needs and help him get his life together. Jimmy came to worship and found people who embraced him, encouraged him and uplifted him. He found people who helped him rededicate himself to a faith in Jesus that he had as a child, but that had diminished because of his sense of letting down his parents and letting down God while engaged in reckless behavior.

Jimmy is now gainfully employed again. He has relocated to his own home, and is positioning himself to be used by God for ministry to others. He worships every Sunday, donates his time each week to help marginalized and disenfranchised people regain their voice and their purpose and is contemplating a call to broader areas of ministry. Looking at Jimmy today, you'd never know he'd fallen on such hard times. Jesus has a way of transforming broken beggars into blessed beggars.

The stories could continue. I could tell you about Michelle, Sam, Jacquie and Brian and many more. Suffice it to say when a group of people decide that they will be a real church in the name of Jesus, life for multitudes of people will never be the same again.

If you are reading this and you are a part of a congregation filled with people who are broken emotionally, socially, spiritually or financially and you are looking for a transformative experience to invade your church, you simply need two things: 1) You need some broken people who have been transformed to start speaking up and telling their stories, and 2) you need to not allow the routine and organization and the "we've never done it this way before" of church life to get in the way. The more that authentic stories are told, the more that transformation will spread.

Early on in my pastorate at Emory, we were having roofing issues. The roof needed to be repaired and the sanctuary painted and a lot of renovation was required. On one particular Saturday, the painting had been completed, but the fumes had been so strong that worshipping in the sanctuary the next day was questionable. Late that night, I made an executive decision, which would later get me in trouble with my trustee board, to hold worship downstairs in the fellowship hall instead of in the sanctuary. There was chaos the next morning because we had never worshipped in the fellowship hall before. Those who had feverishly cleaned up the night before felt that their work wasn't appreciated and the set up for worship was out of sorts. After being told off by several trustees, I decided to open the service with a time of sharing. Figuring that ten or 15 minutes of allowing people to blow off some steam might better prepare us for worship.

> It is when people begging for real church become authentic, transparent and real that true deliverance and true wholeness can come to pass.

Little did I know that the compact environment for worship created an intimate setting. People began to share stories about themselves that they had never shared before. One woman spoke about the challenges and failures that she had experienced in raising her kids. A successful businessman talked about his troubles and shortcomings with managing money. Still another person, highly respected by his country, spoke of his battle with alcohol. Another woman spoke up and asked for prayer for her troubled marriage. What I thought would be a simple 10–15 minute process to clear the air, suddenly turned into an hour and a half of testimony and prayer to the goodness of God in the presence of many trials, tribulations and torments that people were facing. In the midst of personal testimony, we witnessed people connecting in authentic ways. Saying things like:

"I've been worshipping with you for 15 years and never knew that you were going through what you were going through."

"I'm going through what you are going through, perhaps through the grace of God we can get through it together."

"If you had not shared your story today, I don't know if I could have found the strength to deal with what I am dealing with now."

What I witnessed that Sunday was a broken congregation that was beginning to break out of the bondage that the institutional church had placed it in for so long. When we simply tell our stories of what we are going through and what we've been delivered from in the context of community, we will find real church emerging. God has a healing and transformative power for us if we would just be authentic, transparent and real with one another in the name of Jesus.

It is when people begging for real church become authentic, transparent and real that true deliverance and true wholeness can come to pass. If you are begging for it, keep begging. God will make a way somehow.

First Million Dollar Book Profits Will Be Donated to The Beacon Center

A real church is an essential and relevant part of its community. One day, I went to get my clothes out of Tony's Cleaners at the corner of Georgia and Rittenhouse. While I was waiting to be served, I looked out the window back across the street at Emory United Methodist Church and God began revealing a vision of what could be, should be and must be for the residents of the Brightwood community and beyond. At the time, our section of Brightwood was riddled with drug abuse, crack houses, drunkenness, crime, dilapidation and despair. Heroin was sold regularly, that section of Rittenhouse to the side of our church was called "Crack Alley" and the property we owned, in addition to the apartment buildings next to us, was a place where the marginalized and disenfranchised worked out their broken dreams. It was not uncommon for our churchyard to be filled with empty bottles and beer cans, used syringes and condoms. Neither was it uncommon for these articles symbolizing shattered lives to be found in the stairwells of the church building. The smell of urine, on too many occasions, graced the nostrils of those seeking to worship God on Sunday morning. As I stood in Tony's Cleaners on that spring day in 1993, God clearly showed me that He had a much better plan for Emory church, the Brightwood community and all others who would frequent this place. In the dry cleaners, the Lord exposed the fact that the only piece of property we didn't own on the long block of Georgia Avenue between Quackenbos and Rittenhouse were two apartment buildings that at that moment were notorious crack houses. But even more than that, what God revealed was a vision for how a church could play a vital role in the transformation of the disenfranchised community.

The Beacon Center is just one of God's possibilities offered for God's people to live in a prized neighborhood, honored, cherished, revered and affordable to all. That day in the cleaners, God began speaking of what a real church should be all about. A church that not only praises God on Sundays, but a group of people who love their neighbors so much that they would work to meet the needs of those around them 24/7 physically, emotionally, spiritually, relationally and financially. This is real church: when the total needs of a community are met by a people who believe that with Jesus Christ all things are possible.

For those of you who want more details about The Beacon Center, it is a $30 million dollar multipurpose housing, congregational and community development project being launched by the Emory United Methodist Church and its 501(c)(3) community development organization, The Emory Beacon of Light, Inc. The Beacon Center will provide spaces and places to transition people from homelessness to permanent residency. It will provide families and senior citizens with affordable rental housing. It will be a resource for the community through its college-sized indoor multisport space (basketball and soccer), full-service banquet facility, office leasing space, senior citizens services (*e.g.,* optometrist, podiatrist, etc.) and commercial development. All of this will be created around a newly renovated 500-seat sanctuary/community theatre with underground parking.

We look to the Beacon Center to change the landscape of commercial development and the quality of living along Georgia Avenue. More than that, we celebrate the vision that God gave us about what real church looks like in our community.

Endnotes

1 Acts 3:6
2 Matthew 18: 3-5
3 Luke 24: 1-6
4 Matthew 28: 5-7
5 Acts 1:12-14
6 The Sunday after Easter begins a week of revival they call the Simultaneous Revival. It starts on a Sunday evening…every Baptist church in Gary, IN is involved in this experience. Certain preachers are asked to preach community-wide revivals in the morning and noon, and then in the evening each church has its own guest revivalist. It goes from Sunday to Friday. It is outrageous
7 Acts 1: 1-14
8 As the deer pants for streams of water, so my soul pants for you, O God. Psalm 42:1
9 John 21. Specific quote contains verses 15-17.
10 Romans 10:9-10
11 Acts 3: 8-10
12 Mark 12:30-31
13 Acts 2:38
14 John 15:7

authentic. (2009). In Merriam-Webster Online Dictionary, Retrieved June 12, 2009, from http://www.merriam-webster.com/dictionary/authentic

encounter. (2009). In Merriam-Webster Online Dictionary. Retrieved June 12, 2009, from http://www.merriam-webster.com/dictionary/encounter

meaningful. (2009). In Merriam-Webster Online Dictionary. Retrieved June 14, 2009, from http://www.merriam-webster.com/dictionary/meaningful

engagement. (2009). In Merriam-Webster Online Dictionary. Retrieved June 14, 2009, from http://www.merriam-webster.com/dictionary/engagement

radical. (2009). In Merriam-Webster Online Dictionary. Retrieved June 14, 2009, from http://www.merriam-webster.com/dictionary/radical

expectation. (2009). In Merriam-Webster Online Dictionary. Retrieved June 14, 2009, from http://www.merriam-webster.com/dictionary/expectation

Please check out additional,
free downloadable resources for
use with Begging for REAL Church at:
www.beggingforrealchurch.org

There you will find small group guides,
ideas, upcoming events and
information about what's new.

Breinigsville, PA USA
28 April 2010
236938BV00007B/2/P

9 780974 675954